BEYOND THE RAPTURE

An exploration of the three eras prophesied to follow the Rapture by Jesus Christ, King of Kings and Lord of Lords

Denny Bolen

BEYOND THE RAPTURE

COPYRIGHT

© 2014

All rights reserved. No portion of this material may be reproduced without the express consent of the author (who is also the publisher).

ISBN-13:978-1500606473

ISBN-10:1500606472

Scriptural quotes are from the English Standard Version Bible unless otherwise indicated.

Book cover graphics were created by John O'Dell of CardinalGraphics.com

Sixth Edition

Printed by CreateSpace.com

ACKNOWLEDGEMENTS

This book is dedicated to my wonderful wife, Helen, who encouraged me to write and publish it.

My sincere appreciation goes out to a number of people:

John O'Dell (Cardinal Graphics) who worked diligently with me to design the cover for this book. I really appreciate his artistic capabilities.

My brother, Robb, who is a successful author/publisher and has been an inspiration and great help to me.

Diane Eastman who did the first critical edit of this book.

Rex Moses provided pivotal reference material and answered many questions I posed.

To: Jerry Irving who encouraged me to keep going when I was quite discouraged and ready to *throw in the towel*.

Mary Ann Maring and Bob Gariepy who both *went above and beyond* to provide many corrections and suggestions.

Two friends who read and commented on various drafts of the manuscript: Grant Trumbo, and Todd Barnett.

Wayne Derrick, a pastor friend, who answered many questions I posed. He edited the 2d edition for me doing a quite professional job. The introductory paragraphs for each chapter are just one of the important results of his edit.

Kirk Balius, my pastor, who reviewed the overall concepts in this book from a theologian's point of view.

Roy O'Dell, who interviewed me & dedicated an entire podcast of Jazz, Joy & Roy to my authorship of this book.

BEYOND THE RAPTURE

IN HIS ARMS

Denny
2011

Eternity is finally ours
We are caught up to glory
Arrayed before God almighty
We are immersed in love
Wondering but enthralled
Each person wide-eyed
Eager for events to unfold

Our majestic Savior appears
Somehow touching and speaking
to each person alike
Fulfillment at last and
beyond comprehension
Hope is now sight; all are ecstatic

We're barely aware of those around us
Tears and laughter flow simultaneously
All desire to exclaim praises at once
– yet none dare speak
All lips silent until an angel leads us in song
All praise to the Merciful One, we are home.

IN HIS ARMS

PREFACE

The topic of The Rapture and its impact on those left behind seems to have eclipsed interest in what lies beyond for believers. I believe the need for drama and excitement has sidetracked many from what is far more relevant and important! Folks, the excitement and drama unfold with the many marvelous events to occur in the presence of Christ! Too little has been made known about what happens immediately after The Rapture and *above The Tribulation*. We are about to enter into a glorious, everlasting relationship with our marvelous Lord and Savior!

The majority of this book was released in 2012 with the title, *Christ's Spectacular Millennium*. Now I have reframed this book to help Rapture enthusiasts make that needed transition to that which the Bible reveals about the greatest adventure any and every Christian will experience.

Facilitated by the ease of Publish on Demand (POD) and a very user-friendly interface to Kindle, the original book evolved through 12 editions. With this background in mind, the book has been reframed and augmented to describe three distinct periods of time. These eras are as follows:

1.   Above The Tribulation

2.   Christ's 1000 year reign

3.   The New Heavens and Earth

There is sufficient Scripture to describe each era! However the preponderance of verses relate to The Millennium.

BEYOND THE RAPTURE

Jesus' Second Advent begins with His return to Earth. However our heavenly adventure begins with The Rapture. A number of tremendous events occur before The Millennium begins. They are preordained and will be described in the Introduction. All of these are prerequisite to both The Millennium and The New Heavens and Earth. I suspect you will find each of them very exciting.

As I wrote the first book (about The Millennium), my research uncovered what all had to happen first. Whereas I began my quest to discover what The Millennium was about, the necessity of understanding all of these marvelous preliminary events was very profitable to me and hopefully will be to you.

THE MILLENNIUM STUDY

Years back we read (and studied) Randy Alcorn's book, *Heaven*. The thoughts about Heaven were very eye-opening and helpful. However, I became desirous of learning more of what The Millennium might be like, since that is what happens *next* (that is, after the Rapture and the Tribulation).

By way of definition, The Millennium is that prophesied time when our Lord Jesus will literally rule our earth for 1000 years. It is prophesied specifically in the book of Revelation (in chapter 20, in which it is mentioned six times). This reign is mentioned many times in both Old and New Testament (although not designating the specific time period or the name, Millennium). *Millennium*

PREFACE

derives from 2 Latin words: the prefix *mille* means 1000; the suffix *ennium* means annum (or year).

Because I have not found any popular book on the topic, I decided to research and write about this topic with the hope that it would prove enlightening to myself and others. And indeed it has proved quite an exciting journey to research what the Bible and experts have to say about this topic.

I have discovered the reason I had not understood much about the Millennium previously. It is because the Millennium must be *seen* through the lens of what the prophets had to say about the future of Israel. They have specified what God's ultimate and glorious plans are for Israel. To be more specific, it is shown through the record of the covenants and promises God made to Israel long ago.

Just as our Messiah and God's written Word were given to us through Israel, so this great wealth of information about the Millennium is *hidden* in the biblical history of God and Israel! Once this is investigated and understood, then many passages in the New Testament take on *new* meaning as well! This pattern of God revealing Himself through and from Israel continues in and throughout the Millennium. As the Apostle Paul has said, "to the Jew first and also to the Greek!" (cf. Rom. 1:16)

"A larger body of prophetic Scripture is devoted to the subject of the Millennium, developing its character and conditions, than any other one subject."[1]

Some scholars say that The Kingdom is the major theme of the entire Bible.

As I laid out the end-time events and placed them in

their apparent chronological order, it amazed me to discover how perfectly God has intertwined them to accomplish His perfect plan (much of what is revealed in His Word).

Now in the Bible, many of the prophecies about the Millennium begin with or include the phrase, "In that day." It is common practice to accept such as pertaining to the Second Advent. I have utilized these and listed them under Appendix I, Compendium of Millennial Verses.

Although there are over four hundred verses about the Millennium, there are scant verses about Gentiles who enter or are born during this era. Certainly they are a significant part of the Millennium but most of what their lives will be like must be extrapolated or inferred from what is said about Israel and the Jews.

THE NEW HEAVENS AND EARTH STUDY

Originally I had thought descriptions about The Millennium were sufficient to let readers infer what the New Heavens and Earth would be like. Later consideration and study inspired inclusion of an epilogue providing significant information about this era.

MY PURPOSES FOR WRITING THIS BOOK

- Provide a comprehensive look at what all takes place following The Rapture.
- Refocus readers' attention to all the marvelous things God has planned for believers, Israel and planet Earth.

PREFACE

- Remind people of God's eternal love for them.
- Explain the absolute necessity for the Millennium.
- Acquaint readers with God's purposes for the time *Above The Tribulation*, The Millennium and The New Heavens and Earth.
- Address and reduce the mystery of the Millennium.
- Encourage people to think about Christ's Bema Judgment seriously.
- Get people to think beyond the Rapture and get excited about up-coming events.
- Give hope to the dying (and those close to them). Also encourage those who are suffering from a variety of situations not to give in to discouragement but to persevere.
- Reacquaint Christians with God's love for the Jew and Israel.
- Help the reader to understand the significance of post-Rapture events in terms of God's prophecies.
- Show people what we can logically expect in these three eras.
- Take away some of the *fuzziness* people have when trying to differentiate between the Millennium and Heaven.
- Speak to the confusion that is caused by Replacement *Theology*, Amillennialism and Postmillennialism.
- Show that Pretribulationalism is necessary for this view of these eras (as opposed to Posttribulationalism and

Midtribulationalism).

- Cause Christians to realize and consider the great roles we will have in reigning with Christ.
- Help Christians understand what type of beings we will become as the Bride of Christ.
- Embolden Christians not only to witness and do good works, but also to persevere in whatever difficulties they might endure prior to Christ's return.
- Foster awareness of the many wonderful Millennium (kingdom) passages in the Bible.
- Give people hope in these scary times.
- Cause the events following the Rapture, The Millennium and the New Earth to follow to be more realistic and credible to people.
- Provide a primer for those wishing to explore these three eras further .
- Above all, to Glorify God.

---

1 Pentecost, J. Dwight *Things to Come* 47

TABLE OF CONTENTS

ACKNOWLEDGEMENTS .... **iii**
IN HIS ARMS .... **iv**
PREFACE .... **v**
   THE MILLENNIUM STUDY .... *vi*
   THE NEW HEAVENS AND EARTH STUDY .... *viii*
   MY PURPOSES FOR WRITING THIS BOOK .... *viii*
TABLE OF CONTENTS .... **xi**
INTRODUCTION **1**
   ERA 1: JOY ABOVE THE TRIBULATION *1*
   ERA 2: THE MILLENNIUM *2*
   ERA 3: THE NEW HEAVENS AND EARTH *5*
   ENDTIMES *6*
CHAPTER 1 .... **9**
ABOVE THE TRIBULATION **9**
   THE RAPTURE *9*
   BEMA SEAT DESCRIPTION *13*
   THE MARRIAGE OF THE LAMB *17*
   JESUS CHRIST'S SECOND ADVENT *22*
   ISRAEL'S SALVATION *24*
   CHRIST'S VICTORY *25*
   A PROPHESIED GENTILE RESCUE *27*
   NATIONS AND ANGELS JUDGED *28*
   ANTICHRIST'S AND FALSE PROPHET'S FATE *30*
   SATAN BOUND FOR 1000 YEARS *30*
CHAPTER 2 .... **33**

BEYOND THE RAPTURE

MILLENNIUM BEGINNINGS **33**
   MILLENNIUM DISCOURSE *33*
   JESUS INITIATES THE MILLENNIUM *34*
   RESURRECTION OF OT SAINTS *36*
   READINESS *36*
   WEDDING SUPPER OF THE LAMB *37*
   THE CORONATION OF CHRIST *39*
   INTRODUCTION OF THE BRIDE *44*
CHAPTER 3 .... **47**
THE NEW JERUSALEM **47**
   OUR HEAVENLY HOME *48*
   LIFE IN NEW JERUSALEM *50*
   NEW JERUSALEM'S EXTERIOR *51*
   NEW JERUSALEM'S INTERIOR *52*
   NEW JERUSALEM CONTROVERSY *53*
   NEW JERUSALEM'S LOCATION *54*
   OUR TRAVELS *57*
CHAPTER 4 .... **59**
CHRIST'S KINGDOM **59**
   MILLENNIAL JERUSALEM *59*
   THE TEMPLE *61*
   SURROUNDINGS *64*
   TEMPLE WORSHIP *64*
   KINGDOM WORSHIP *66*
   CHRIST'S REIGN *67*
   CHRIST'S WORLD DESIGN *69*

TABLE OF CONTENTS

EARLY ACTIVITIES OF THE RESURRECTED 71
CHAPTER 5 75
BRIDE SAINTS 75
   IMMEASURABLE JOY 75
   NEW IMMORTAL BODIES 77
   OUR NEW SPIRITUAL PERSONALITIES 79
   MARRIAGE SURPASSED 80
   INTIMACY 81
   OUR CAPABILITES 82
   OUR FELLOWSHIP 83
   ANGELS 85
   OUR MINISTRIES 86
   INTERACTIONS WITH MORTALS 86
   INTERACTIONS AS RULERS 87
   INTERACTIONS AS JUDGES 88
   INTERACTIONS AS PRIESTS 88
   BRIDE SAINTS OVERALL MINISTRY 89
CHAPTER 6 91
ISRAEL 91
   REPLACEMENT "THEOLOGY" 96
   WORSHIP IN ISRAEL 97
   ISRAEL'S GRATITUDE 99
   GOD'S COVENANTS 99
   ISRAEL'S PEOPLE 100
   JEWISH DEMOGRAPHICS 101
   NOTABLE OT SAINTS 102

BEYOND THE RAPTURE

CHAPTER 7 .... **105**
PURPOSES AND BENEFITS OF THE MILLENNIUM **105**
- *PURPOSES* *105*
- *BENEFITS* *109*

CHAPTER 8 .... **111**
WORSHIP IN JESUS' KINGDOM **111**
- *WORSHIP* *111*
- *MORTALS' RELATIONSHIP TO JESUS* *112*
- *THE CHURCH* *115*
- *POTENTIAL CELEBRATION OF THE 7 FEAST DATES IN THE MILLENNIUM* *117*
- *SABBATH ACTIVITIES* *121*
- *PROGRESSIVE REVELATION* *121*
- *RIGHTEOUSNESS ENFORCED* *121*
- *THE HOLY SPIRIT* *122*
- *RITUALS* *123*
- *MUSIC* *125*

CHAPTER 9 .... **127**
LIFE IN CHRIST'S KINGDOM **127**
- *MORTALS* *127*
- *POPULATION* *128*
- *GOVERNMENT* *129*
- *GOD'S BELOVED ISRAEL* *131*
- *PAX CHRISTUS* *132*
- *MORALITY* *136*
- *SOCIETY* *138*
- *HUMANITY* *139*

TABLE OF CONTENTS

ANIMALS	*140*
VOCATIONS	*142*
EDUCATION	*142*
SCIENCE	*143*
ENTERTAINMENT	*144*
BIRTHDAYS	*146*
HEALTH	*147*
WEATHER	*147*
CHAPTER 10	**149**
FINAL EVENTS	**149**
END OF THE MILLENIUM	*149*
THE GREAT WHITE THRONE	*153*
EPILOGUE	**157**
THE NEW HEAVENS AND EARTH	**157**
ODE TO CHRIST'S REIGN	**161**
APPENDIX	**165**
A. BIRTH PANGS	**165**
OLIVET DISCOURSE	*165*
SIGNS OF THE TIMES	*167*
PROPHECY FULFILMENT	*167*
ISRAEL'S ENEMIES	*170*
ISRAEL'S CURRENT DILEMMA	*172*
ANTI-SEMITISM	*174*
EARTHQUAKES	*176*
EARTHQUAKE DATA	*176*
B. PROGRESSIVE REVELATION	**179**
INTRODUCTION	*179*

BEYOND THE RAPTURE

- *DISPENSATIONS* *181*
- *DISPENSATIONS CHART* *182*
- **C. MARY'S FAMILY** **183**
  - *JESUS' BIRTH* *183*
  - *THE FLIGHT TO EGYPT* *184*
  - *LIFE IN NAZARETH* *185*
  - *JESUS' MINISTRY* *186*
  - *THE CRUCIFIXION* *187*
  - *JOSEPH* *187*
- **D. SPIRITUAL BEINGS** **189**
  - *ANGELS* *189*
  - *JESUS* *191*
  - *THE HUMAN SOUL (SPIRIT)* *193*
- **E. ANCIENT JEWISH WEDDING PRACTICES** **197**
  - *MARRIAGE COVENANT AND BRIDE PRICE* *197*
  - *THE CUP* *197*
  - *GIFTS FOR THE BRIDE* *198*
  - *MIKVEH* *198*
  - *PREPARING A PLACE* *198*
  - *WAITING BRIDE CONSECRATED* *198*
  - *BRIDEGROOM FETCHES HIS BRIDE* *199*
  - *7 DAYS IN THE WEDDING CHAMBER* *199*
  - *MARRIAGE SUPPER* *199*
  - *DEPART FOR HOME* *199*
  - *PARALLELS TO CHRIST AND THE CHURCH* *200*
- **F. MY "PROPHECY" TESTIMONY** **203**

TABLE OF CONTENTS

THE GOSPEL 205
G. ORDER OF END-TIMES EVENT CHART 207
H. THEORETICAL GOVERNMENT MODEL 209
   NATIONS JUDGED 209
   RULERS 210
   RIGHTEOUSNESS ENFORCED 211
I. COMPENDIUM OF END-TIME VERSES 213
   "IN THAT DAY" VERSES 213
   TRIBULATION VERSES 213
J. STUDY OF GOD'S FINAL 3 ERAS 215
   ABOVE THE TRIBULATION 215
      RAPTURE RESURRECTION 215
      THE RAPTURE 215
      THE BEMA JUDGMENT 216
      THE WEDDING OF THE LAMB 216
      RESCUE OF ISRAEL 217
      CHRIST'S JUDGMENTS 217
      RESURRECTIONS 217
   MILLENNIUM 217
      NT BOOK FOCUS 217
      OT BOOK FOCUS 218
   NEW HEAVENS AND EARTH 219
   STUDY APPROACH 219
   FINAL THOUGHTS 220
K. MILLENNIUM SONGS 221
   JOY TO THE WORLD 221
   ALL HAIL THE POWER OF JESUS' NAME 222
L. THE TRIBULATION: GOD'S PURPOSES, Satan's Plot & Tribulation Events Chart 223

GOD'S PURPOSES	*223*
Satan's Plot	*223*
ABOUT THE AUTHOR	**225**
STATEMENT OF FAITH	*225*
ENDNOTES	**227**
CAST OF "CHARACTERS"	*227*
ABBREVIATIONS	*228*
NOTES	*228*
RECOMMENDED READING	*230*
GLOSSARY	**231**
BIBLIOGRAPHY	**237**
BOOKS	*237*
ARTICLE	*238*
BIBLES	*238*
INTERNET	*238*
ANCILLARY QUOTE	*239*
SCRIPTURE REFERENCES	**241**

INTRODUCTION

Our Lord has extraordinary events planned for us beginning with the Rapture. I will mention them here and then reveal the marvelous details later as they *occur* within this book. So first let me present the broad picture in terms of three eras. They are:

Era 1: Joy above the Tribulation
(The Marriage and Honeymoon of the Lamb)

Era 2: The 1000 year reign of Christ (The Millennium) and the major focus of this book;

Era 3: The eternal New Heavens and Earth (described in the Epilogue).

As I mentioned, each era has its distinct and astoundingly wondrous events. I hope you are increasingly intrigued as we explore every nuance of these tremendous times in which every believer will exult.

ERA 1: JOY ABOVE THE TRIBULATION

It is more than ironic that while the people on earth are suffering the wrath of God and the manipulations of Satan, those raptured and resurrected will be experiencing indescribable ecstasy.

The components of this seven-year era (primarily above the fray) are:

- The Resurrection
- The Rapture
- The Bema Seat Judgment

BEYOND THE RAPTURE

- The Marriage of the Lamb
- The Honeymoon
- The Rescue of Israel
- The Judgment of Nations and individuals
- The resurrection of Tribulation martyrs and OT saints
- The preparation of Earth for the Millennium

The Rapture is an intriguing topic. This marvelous event *catapults* the last NT saints into Jesus' arms instantaneously – just before the Tribulation (allowing them to cheat death). Believers will not only escape death but many horrendous situations such as persecution, tragic illnesses (or handicaps) and other intolerable situations.

Although I am not beset with such a situation, I desire to be among those raptured (maranatha!), and am quite curious as to what happens next!

NOTE: I mention persecution above due to the fact that currently, there are more Christians being persecuted than in all of history. Estimates of the number of Christians being martyred currently range from 100 to 200 thousand per year. The average matches Hal Lindsey's posted 150,000 per year (12,500 per month, 411 per day).

ERA 2: THE MILLENNIUM

People long for utopia and have long sought paradise conditions. It can never happen until Jesus reigns! Jesus' disciples, and later throngs of people on Palm Sunday, sought after a perfect kingdom from Jesus. Theoretically it could have come to them at that time, but Israel's religious

INTRODUCTION

and political leaders rejected their Messiah and had Him put to death.

Multitudes of Jews have subsisted spiritually and suffered horrifically down through the ages for rejecting their Messiah and invoking their own curse by saying "His blood be upon our heads and upon our children's." (Mat. 27:25) Yet by God's grace, myriads of Gentiles have profited immeasurably from their calamitous decision.

Since early in my Christian life, I have taken an interest in End-Time prophecy and the pertinent events which have taken place in just my lifetime. There has been much ado about the Tribulation and especially The Rapture. Yet I find it curious that there has been so little discourse about The Millennium; I have discovered that it is the most prominent prophetic topic in the Bible.

In the preface, I mentioned that there are 400 plus verses about the Millennium in the Bible (mostly in the OT). To highlight this incredible era appropriately, I will list the extent to which The Millennium is described by all of the major prophets and most of the minor prophets. The quantity of these verses speak of just how significant the Millennium is in terms of God's promises to Israel (and to us, The Church, as well). We also can see how such could not possibly relate to The Church (contrary to Replacement Theology concepts).

Three of the major prophets and one minor prophet contain whole chapters relating to Christ's Second Advent with significant focus on the Millennium. Daniel and nine of the minor prophets also speak of the Second Advent and Millennium. In addition, there is much in the book of Psalms. The minor prophets excluded are: Jonah, Nahum and Habbakuk. Again, to impress you of the significance of The Millennium and its overall importance to both Israelis and The Church, let me list the number of complete chapters dedicated to The Millennium in the Bible: there are nineteen Psalms; Isaiah has ten chapters, Jeremiah – three, Ezekiel – fourteen, and Zechariah – two. That makes 48 chapters dedicated to the Millennium. You will find specific data about this in Appendix J, *Study of God's Final 3 Eras*.

The majority of Evangelicals are unaware of these all important facts. Sadly I was at the top of the list for having been ignorant of this information. I don't understand how I glossed over it repeatedly when the concepts infuse so much of the OT. I have been reading a chapter of the Bible daily much of my life as a Christian (since 1970, alternating between NT & OT.). And yet I remained uninformed about the Millennium for decades! Hopefully this book makes up for that oversight to some degree.

Even with all this Scripture dedicated to the topic, there is still a certain silence about much of Millennium activities. I am filling some of the gaps in what I imagine Christ's reign might be like. Do understand that unless I quote Scripture or a Bible scholar to back my assertions, the ideas expressed are mine (based on familiarity with Biblical concepts, logic and sometimes pure imagination). To the degree possible, I have based my ideas on Scripture or Scriptural concepts. In Revelation, we find a brief description of the Millennium:

> Then I saw thrones, and seated on them were those to whom the authority to judge was committed. Also I saw the souls of those who had been beheaded for the testimony of Jesus and for the word of God, and those who had not

INTRODUCTION

worshiped the beast or its image and had not received its mark on their foreheads or their hands. They came to life and reigned with Christ for a thousand years. This is the first resurrection. Blessed and holy is the one who shares in the first resurrection! Over such the second death has no power, but they will be priests of God and of Christ, and they will reign with him for a thousand years. (Rev. 20:4–6)

Because the previous verses pertain to the Tribulation martyred saints, here are verses about the church in general:

For you (*Jesus*) were slaughtered, and your blood has ransomed people for God from every tribe and language and people and nation. And you have caused them to become a Kingdom of priests for our God. And they will reign on the earth. (Rev. 5:9b–10 NLT)

During this era (the Millennium), I believe Jesus will honor His Bride (the church) in incredible ways.

More than all other nations, God will honor the Jews and the land of Israel. This is addressed in depth later.

First and foremost however, the primary purpose of the Millennium is that Christ Jesus is exalted, glorified and worshipped. The chapter entitled Purpose and Benefits of the Millennium shows twenty-two more purposes for the Millennium.

ERA 3: THE NEW HEAVENS AND EARTH

As marvelous as The Millennium will be, the New Heavens and Earth will surpass it. There will be no sin, no sorrow, and no death – just unending joy in righteousness. Scripture and *Bible logic* dictate the other qualities and aspects described in the New Heaven and Earth Synopsis.

BEYOND THE RAPTURE

ENDTIMES

From any number of perspectives, it appears we are living in the last days. I, for one, believe we are beginning to experience the birth pangs leading to the Tribulation, described by Jesus in the Olivet Discourse (cf. Mat. 24:1–51, Mark 13:1–37, Luke 17:20–37)

Large scale earthquakes are increasing significantly, the Roman Empire appears to be revived with the European Union and Israel's enemies are growing in strength and determination. Israel is becoming more and more isolated. The noose is being tightened around her proverbial neck.

Hal Lindsey has summed up the world situation this way in his Internet news letter (January 6, 2012): "From Iran to Iraq to Syria to Egypt to Europe to Russia to North Korea to the United States, Bob Dylan would observe, 'The times they are a-changin.' But more than just the times, changes are coming fast and furiously to governments, economies, societies, religious communities, in fact, entire nations. Upheaval seems to be the order of the day; uncertainty and fear its most common results." [1]

"Through environmental, social, financial, national, religious and agricultural disasters, God is sounding the alarm . . . As the signs of the end of the age and of His return are increasing in frequency and intensity, there is still time not only to embrace the hope that God promises, but to offer it to someone else." [2]

God is giving Christians and the world a great display of His splendor by fulfilling many prophecies *right before our eyes.* Beginning with the reestablishment of Israel in

INTRODUCTION

1948, He has set Israel into a precarious state. On one hand, they are back in their land (per Ezekiel's prophecy) but on the other, the countries specified by prophecy are arrayed against them. He is setting the stage for the Second Advent in obvious ways that are both exciting and terrifying.

Thus God has already drawn Israel's destined enemies into battle position against her and set the stage to allow the Antichrist to accomplish his sham rescue of Israel. Her enemies are *rattling their swords* so loudly that the entire world is becoming nervous. This appears to be a precursor to the fulfillment of this verse: following

> I am going to make Jerusalem a cup that sends all the surrounding peoples reeling. (Zec. 12:2a)

Jesus berated the Pharisees for failing to recognize their Messiah at His first appearance.

> Jesus also said to the crowds, "When you see a cloud rising in the west, you say at once, 'A shower is coming.' And so it happens. And when you see the south wind blowing, you say, 'There will be scorching heat,' and it happens. You hypocrites! You know how to interpret the appearance of earth and sky, but why do you not know how to interpret the present time?" (Luke 12:54–56)

I would encourage you to be aware of the signs of His imminent return, although I do not think the *pangs* have ratcheted up to what they will be just before the Rapture. *Please see Appendix A, Birth Pangs, for details.*

Please realize and remember that this book is focused primarily on the Rapture, The Millennium and the New Heavens and Earth. It includes little about what happens on earth during the Tribulation.

BEYOND THE RAPTURE

1. Lindsey, January 6, 2012

2. Lotz, Anne Graham February 27, 2012

CHAPTER 1

ABOVE THE TRIBULATION

From the chapter's title, you can guess that this is not going to be a discussion about the horrific things the people of earth are about to suffer. Instead we have the privilege of exploring the immeasurable joys that the Bride of Christ will experience above the devastation.

I am writing this book from a perspective usually described as premillennial and pretribulational. These are belief in the following sequence of events: **First**, the Rapture, **Second**, the Tribulation and **Third**, Christ's return to earth to initiate the Millennium,

At His Second Advent Jesus will personally usher in the Millennium as He establishes His promised kingdom rule on Earth. The term pretribulational means that we expect our Lord to remove all living believers from the Earth prior to a prophesied seven year period known as the Tribulation (please reference Appendix L, THE TRIBULATION: GOD'S PURPOSES, Satan's Plot and EVENTS CHART). The Tribulation events examined in this chapter include events in Heaven and events on Earth. The spectacular removal of believers from the earth is called the Rapture.

THE RAPTURE

As I stated above, I believe that the Rapture will occur before the Tribulation. In other words, saints (believers) living just before the Tribulation will be caught up to

BEYOND THE RAPTURE

Heaven, along with all who had previously *died in Christ*.

> For the Lord himself will descend from Heaven with a cry of command, with the voice of an archangel, and with the sound of the trumpet of God. And the dead in Christ will rise first. Then we who are alive, who are left, will be caught up together with them in the clouds to meet the Lord in the air, and so we will always be with the Lord. (1The. 4:16–17)

Let us consider what happens during The Rapture forgetting what happens to those left behind and focusing on what happens to believers. Those raptured have either escaped earth and cheated death or been resurrected from the dead (some having waited 2000 years for theirs).

Each receives a glorious new body and is fully alive in ways we can't even imagine. The Bible provides no clue as to how Jesus clusters us once there. There could be billions of us. Yet I believe Jesus in His kindness will gather us with those we have been closest to on earth.

Regardless of those surrounding us, we will be primarily focused on our Lord who will somehow be available to each believer. In the ancient Jewish wedding tradition, the groom came for His bride (by surprise in the middle of the night) with a celebrative wedding party. We're given no clue who that might be for the rapture. Candidates are God the Father and the Holy Spirit plus myriad angels. They won't be Old Testament saints (they're resurrected later). The logistics of all this are beyond comprehension but God will accomplish this *once in-the history of the world* event wonderfully amidst great joy and fulfillment.

ABOVE THE TRIBULATION

One aspect of our finding ourselves in Heaven with Jesus will be our newly acquired and incredible immortal bodies. Although being in Heaven with Christ, family and friends will be foremost in our experience, we will begin noticing one another's spectacular new bodies and then perhaps lastly our own bodies. Our Lord promised us the eternal bodies through His Scriptures. Now that we're with Him, we are made wonderfully aware of not only our bodies but the instantaneous fulfillment of His many promises: eternal life, being in His presence, being in Heaven and having new bodies that are perfect and sinless. Many of those receiving such bodies left behind bodies that were painfully crippled or limited. These might appreciate the transition even more so.

As I pondered the Rapture, I wondered how Jesus would change our bodies (just to survive the trip, you know) – things such as extreme cold, no oxygen and no gravity (for starters). This caused me to consider some very pertinent portions of Scripture:

> And we are eagerly waiting for him to return as our Savior. He will take our weak mortal bodies and change them into glorious bodies like his own, using the same power with which he will bring everything under his control. (Php. 3:20c–21 NLT)

> "How are the dead raised? With what kind of body do they come?" What you sow does not come to life unless it dies. And what you sow is not the body that is to be, but a bare kernel, perhaps of wheat or of some other grain. But God gives it a body as he has chosen ... There are heavenly bodies and earthly bodies, but the glory of the heavenly is of one kind, and the glory of the earthly is of another.

BEYOND THE RAPTURE

(1 Cor. 15:35b–40)

So is it with the resurrection of the dead. What is sown is perishable; what is raised is imperishable; ... It is sown a natural body; it is raised a spiritual body... (1 Cor. 15:42, 44)

The first man was from the earth, a man of dust; the second man is from Heaven ... Just as we have borne the image of the man of dust, we shall also bear the image of the man of Heaven. (1 Cor. 15:47, 49)

Flesh and blood cannot inherit the kingdom of God, nor does the perishable inherit the imperishable. (1 Cor. 15:50b)

Paul next describes the Rapture and ties in these concepts:

In a moment, in the twinkling of an eye, at the last trumpet. For the trumpet will sound, and the dead will be raised imperishable, and we shall be changed. For this perishable body must put on the imperishable, and this mortal body must put on immortality. (1 Cor. 15:52–53)

Unfortunately the Rapture has been overly stressed and a most important event almost overlooked. I am referring to the **resurrection of the church**. All believers who died before the rapture will receive their eternal bodies at that time! Some souls will have waited nearly 2000 years for this event!

When we are raptured, our bodies will be transformed from bodies of flesh into immortal bodies. These bodies will probably be very similar to Christ's in His post-resurrection appearance. That is, Jesus appeared to the disciples senses as *fully human* (Thomas was able to touch His wounds), yet He demonstrated supernatural abilities such as appearing suddenly in their midst. *Read*

ABOVE THE TRIBULATION

2Corinthians 5:1–9 for further perspective about how our bodies will be changed.

> For we long for our bodies to be released from sin and suffering. We, too, wait with eager hope for the day when God will give us our full rights as his adopted children, including the new bodies he has promised us. (Rom. 8:23c NLT)

I have wondered if those who were cremated might not be able to be resurrected. However, in pondering the whole burial situation, I realized that during the millennia before modern-day embalming, bodies were just put in a box, buried and allowed to *turn to dust.* God provided each of us a DNA and genome which governs our body's development and maintenance. I am certain, He has all of that information *cataloged* and is waiting to reuse that information as He provides each person his or her resurrection body.

The idea of preparing for The Rapture is a rather illusive concept. We are encouraged to look forward to His return. But in our day-to-day life, we should be living as though He could return at any time for another reason. None of us knows when we will expire and meet Jesus. How long anyone of us gets to live is a mystery. Preparedness is key.

BEMA SEAT DESCRIPTION

I dare not attempt to describe what happens immediately after the rapture beyond my opening poem. I would hope Jesus would greet each person face-to-face and touch us in some endearing manner. However He greets us, it will be the beginning of an existence of ecstatic joy for each believer.

I do believe two infinitely important events will soon follow The Rapture: the Bema Seat Judgment and the Wedding of the Lamb (in that order).

Bema is not a word normally used in English. It is a Greek word associated with the Greek games. The Bema was the three-level podium upon which the winner and two runner-ups stood (with the winner on the highest tier in the middle). The Apostle Paul has used it with regards to Christ's giving of rewards to believers. The timing of the Bema is indicated by Luke 14:14 and Revelation 19:7–8.

> When you give a banquet, invite the poor, the crippled, the lame, the blind, and you will be blessed. Although they cannot repay you, **you will be repaid at the resurrection of the righteous.** (Luke 14:14 NIV)

The resurrection of the righteous (from the Church Age) occurs at the Rapture. That the rewards of the righteous are given during the tribulation is further bolstered by Revelation 19:8. It renders "righteousness of the saints" as plural such that it is not the righteousness of Christ.

> His bride has made herself ready. Fine linen, bright and clean, was given her to wear (Fine linen stands for the righteous acts of God's holy people.). (Rev. 19:7d–8 NIV)

The following passage describes the Bema Seat event:

> For we must all appear and be revealed as we are before the judgment seat of Christ, so that each one may receive [his pay] according to what he has done in the body, whether good or evil [considering what his purpose and motive have been, and what he has achieved, been busy with, and given himself and his attention to accomplishing]. (2Cor. 5:10 AMP)

ABOVE THE TRIBULATION

NOTE: The lengthy rendition of this verse is to aid understanding

For Christians, this will be the *second most important* event in their eternal life; the most important being, *trusting Christ*. The Bema will echo forever how faithfully each Christian served God (on earth).

> For God is not unjust. He will not forget how hard you have worked for him and how you have shown your love to him by caring for other believers, as you still do. Our great desire is that you will keep on loving others as long as life lasts, in order to make certain that what you hope for will come true. (Heb. 6:10–11 NLT)

Our lives will be evaluated by Jesus, Himself. Our behavior and deeds will be scrutinized. That which pleased Him will be rewarded throughout eternity. Whatever we did in His name wrongly or carnal acts on our part will cause us significant eternal loss. This is better explained in 1 Corinthians 3.

> For no one can lay a foundation other than that which is laid, which is Jesus Christ. Now if anyone builds on the foundation with gold, silver, precious stones, wood, hay, straw – each one's work will become manifest, for the Day will disclose it, because it will be revealed by fire, and the fire will test what sort of work each one has done. If the work that anyone has built on the foundation survives, he will receive a reward. If anyone's work is burned up, he will suffer loss, though he himself will be saved, but only as through fire... (1 Cor. 3:11–15)

Some of the most highly rewarded people might be missionaries, church planters, the martyred and the persecuted. Lest I give the wrong impression, I should say the rewards are given for how faithfully we served Christ in accordance with the giftedness and life situation we are given. Some of the least rewarded might be fallen, unrepentant Christian leaders and consistently carnal Christians. A parable which Jesus told about talents illustrates both the idea of rewards and the lack thereof. It is lengthy, so please refer to Matthew 25:14–30. Jesus says we will be both rulers and priests with him. I infer this from Jesus' words, "I'll put you in charge of many things . . . ," that this is linked to our future capacity in either of those roles.

In Scripture, five different crowns are mentioned as rewards from God.

1. A Crown of Life: for patiently enduring testing and temptations (cf. Jam. 1:12)
2. An Imperishable Crown for practicing self-control in everything. (cf. 1 Cor. 9:25)
3. A Crown of joyousness for soul winning (cf. 1 The. 2:19)
4. A Crown of glory and honor unending for elders who shepherded their flock well (cf. 1Pet.5:4)
5. A Crown of righteousness for those who eagerly anticipated His appearing (cf. 2Tim. 4:8)

As believers our chief motivation for Christian living and service ought to be a desire to see God glorified, especially as an expression of thanksgiving for all He has done on our behalf. However, the Bible unapologetically speaks of rewards that believers have a right to expect for faithful service. Paul certainly uses this as a motivation and encouragement to right living in his closing words in 1 Corinthians 15.

> So, my dear brothers and sisters, be strong and immovable. Always work enthusiastically for the Lord, for you know that nothing you do for the Lord is ever useless. (1 Cor. 15:58)

Missionary Jim Elliott was martyred by the very people he came to save in Ecuador in 1956. Yet many in that tribe, including some who participated in the spearing, later came to Christ by the ministry of Jim's widow, Elizabeth. His attitude towards serving our Lord was well summarized in this phrase found in one of his journals: "He is no fool who gives up what he cannot keep to gain that which he cannot lose." [1]

Another Scripture pertinent to the Bema will be "to those whom much has been given, much is expected." (Luke 12:48)

THE MARRIAGE OF THE LAMB

Once we have each withstood the rigors and gained the rewards of the Bema Seat Judgment, the next event to unfold will be the Marriage of the Lamb. This grand event is the greatly anticipated culmination for all Christians. Jesus, himself, awaits us with great longing.

> For I feel a divine jealousy for you, since I betrothed you to one husband, to present you as a pure virgin to Christ. (2Cor. 11:2)

Also reference Ephesians 5:27, Psalm 45 and Matthew 22:1-14.

The Marriage of the Lamb will probably take place during the time of the Tribulation. Christians who comprise *His Bride* will experience joy and fulfillment unimaginably wondrous.

BEYOND THE RAPTURE

> Then I heard what seemed to be the voice of a great multitude, like the roar of many waters and like the sound of mighty peals of thunder, crying out,
>
> "Hallelujah! For the Lord our God the Almighty reigns. Let us rejoice and exult and give him the glory, for the marriage of the Lamb has come, and his Bride has made herself ready;
>
> It was granted her to clothe herself with fine linen, bright and pure" – for the fine linen is the righteous deeds of the saints." (Rev. 19:6–8)

One question that comes to mind is, "Since earth is being *battered* during the Tribulation, where might the wedding take place?" In light of the Bible passages regarding this topic, the most logical place is the New Jerusalem. In ancient weddings, the wedding chamber was created within the house of the groom's father. After honeymoon and the marriage supper, the groom took the bride to a separate home; one he had prepared. Please reference Appendix E, Ancient Jewish Wedding Practices.

I infer that we will be cloistered with our Savior in a very spectacular place within New Jerusalem during the Tribulation. Then after the Wedding Supper on Earth, Jesus will escort us to our new dwellings He has prepared throughout The New Jerusalem.

> One of the seven angels ... said to me, "Come, I will show you the bride, the wife of the Lamb." And he carried me away in the Spirit to a mountain great and high, and showed me the Holy City, Jerusalem, coming down out of Heaven from God. It shone with the glory of God, and its brilliance was like that of a very precious jewel, like a jasper, clear as crystal. (Rev. 21:9–11 NIV)

Will there be a wedding ceremony? In the ancient Jewish wedding the groom showed up *unexpectedly* in the middle of the night and took his bride to his wedding chamber and they remained there a week. After that there was a ceremonial celebration with waiting groomsmen, bridesmaids, friends and relatives that could last for days. In the case of the Wedding of The Lamb, there could be a ceremony to initiate the wedding and it would involve the most significant beings in our universe: Jesus, God the Father, the Holy Spirit, myriads of heavenly hosts and the multitudes who comprise the Bride of Christ.

What ceremony, music and pronouncements that might occur are never defined in Scripture. Our God could dazzle us with much grandeur to heighten and commemorate the experience. Such thoughts evoke the magnificent descriptions of God's throne in the Book of Revelation.

The oriental wedding wonderfully depicts the Marriage of the Lamb. It involves a sequence of events and is described in detail in Appendix E. Ancient Jewish Wedding Practices. There are six events in this ritual: 1) the marriage contract; 2) the preparation; 3) spiriting away the bride; 4) the marriage; 5) the honeymoon and 6) the marriage supper (celebration). Contrary to our traditions, the groom is the central focus of such a wedding; this is so superbly appropriate for our Lord.

Once the ceremony is concluded we will enter into our wondrously enhanced relationship with Jesus. Whereas a human marriage encompasses commitment, romance and sexual consummation; the Marriage of the Lamb will be a glorious spiritual union between all Church Age believers and Christ. So to meet our Lord face to face and become His, entirely and eternally, will be consummation of our earthly faith and hope.

BEYOND THE RAPTURE

Of Jesus' many names, He chose *Lamb* for this occasion. So we may assume His relationship with us will be gentle and not intimidating. An earthly lamb is sweet, cuddly and playful. These qualities do not seem appropriate for our Lord. The sacrificial role of our Lamb does. But Scripture indicates Jesus will return as the Lion of Judah, so the title Lamb would simply indicate His all loving and adoring role toward His Bride.

A question naturally arises regarding the reason Jesus would want such a close relationship with the likes of us? Scripture answers this question:

> Even before he made the world, God loved us and chose us in Christ to be holy and without fault in his eyes. God decided in advance to adopt us into his own family by bringing us to himself through Jesus Christ. This is what he wanted to do, and it gave him great pleasure. So we praise God for the glorious grace he has poured out on us who belong to his dear Son. (Eph 1:4-6)

The ancient Jewish wedding was a time of face-to-face intimacy and joy. And whereas there will be billions of believers, each will commune with Jesus – seeing Him, touching Him, hearing and speaking to Him and He them. To have an instantaneous, continuous, and intimate relationship with our Lord throughout eternity will elevate a love relationship in which we will exult forever. To know His thoughts, emotions and desires and to experience His total love and knowledge of us will be incredible. There will probably be seven years of wondrous uninterrupted communion with our Lord before the Millennium begins

Jesus will exhibit His marvelous capability to interact with each of us simultaneously. Note that He already did this during all of the Church Age. Having upheld the entire universe by the power of His Word, this is a small but tremendous capability that He will employ. He will do this in interaction with the incredible new capabilities our resurrection bodies will possess.

It is difficult to comprehend what this will mean to our Lord. Yet we can extrapolate from the preceding verse in Ephesians 1:5 ... it gave Him *(God)* great pleasure to choose us in Christ, make us holy and adopt us into His own family. So for our Lord Jesus to experience His plans and prophecies being fulfilled in this wedding (and throughout the Millennium) will give Him great joy!

I should imagine this will be a time of intense dialogue as well of just being, that is quietly experiencing Jesus to the fullest. Perhaps as the intensity of all this calms to a degree, we will begin to be more aware of those around us. Whether we will have that ability to communicate with many simultaneously is unknown. But we will be aware of our loved ones from the past, renew old acquaintances and far more.

All the NT heroes will be part of this Heavenly congregation including the Apostles and authors of the New Testament. All NT notables will avail themselves to us. The overall thrills, joy and fulfillment will be on a scale we cannot possibly fathom. All of us will exist and commune in complete perfection and righteousness.

Think of it – in a short amount of time we will each have done the following:

- Either escaped earth and cheated death or been resurrected from the dead
- Received our glorious new bodies

BEYOND THE RAPTURE

- Received our rewards
- Became fully united with Christ
- Became reunited with all of our Christian friends and family.
- Became acquainted with the heroes of the faith personally

Nothing we might imagine could be more thrilling, joyful and fulfilling than this.

It is overwhelming just to try to conceive of such a time. Yet this is our eternal hope; this is what God has promised. This is the culmination of all our aspirations, dreams and faith. This is why so many sacrificed for God. Glory be to Him for what He's soon to do.

And not to take away from the revelry of these thoughts but this is only the beginning of many experiences and adventures we will have with our Lord for eternity. All of these activities were foreordained by God. This incredible act of grace and mercy crowns Him anew with glory and majesty. He is pleased to draw us into this intimate relationship with Himself. The grace and mercy shown us defies logic as we know it. Each and every saint will be eternally grateful. We do know that God is such a God of love that He still desires relationship with mankind despite all our failures to love and serve Him as He desired.

JESUS CHRIST'S SECOND ADVENT

So far, I have touched on some significant and glorious events which take place in heaven during the Tribulation. These were described because, as will be seen later, they relate directly to events in the Millennium. During this time, however, things are frightful on earth. It is beyond the scope and purpose of this book to delve into this horrendous period in detail. One may read for himself a detailed description in the book of Revelation, as chapters 6–19 relate prophetically what will unfold. The prophet Joel gives an overview in his third chapter. I like the way one author segues the shift from the heavenly scenes to the earthly ones.

"While the saints are in Heaven preparing to return with Christ, the armies of the earth gather and move toward Jerusalem, inspired and led by Satan, the Antichrist and False Prophet who have deceived the nations." [2]

> Proclaim this among the nations: Consecrate for war; stir up the mighty men. Let all the men of war draw near; let them come up. Beat your plowshares into swords, and your pruning hooks into spears; let the weak say, "I am a warrior."
>
> Hasten and come, all you surrounding nations, and gather yourselves there. Bring down your warriors, O LORD. Let the nations stir themselves up and come up to the Valley of Jehoshaphat; for there I will sit to judge all the surrounding nations
>
> Put in the sickle, for the harvest is ripe. Go in, tread, for the winepress is full. The vats overflow, for their evil is great.
>
> Multitudes, multitudes, in the valley of decision! For the day of the LORD is near in the valley of decision. The sun and the moon are darkened, and the stars withdraw their shining. The LORD roars from Zion, and utters his voice from Jerusalem, and the heavens and the earth quake. But the LORD is a refuge to his people, a stronghold to the people of Israel. (Joel 3:9–16)

BEYOND THE RAPTURE

ISRAEL'S SALVATION

The nation of Israel is the focal point of the Tribulation events, as Satan accelerates his efforts to destroy God's chosen nation. But this only sets the stage for God's miraculous delivery of Israel and the mass conversion of its people when they turn to Jesus.

Aside: It is difficult for believers to comprehend how resolutely Jews (living both in or outside Israel) has resisted the Gospel for many hundreds of years. During The Tribulation the 144,000 Jewish evangelists will roam the earth winning souls to Christ. However there is nothing in Scripture to indicate how they might impact their fellow Jews. Could it be that God uses them to prepare their hearts for their Messiah?.

Following is one author's description of Christ's marvelous rescue and salvation of Israel.

"As the armies of the Earth gather, Israel finally realizes the rejected Messiah of Isaiah 53 and Daniel 9:26, Jesus Christ, is their only hope! Israel now calls out to Jesus Christ with a heart of supplication and repentance, acknowledging their errors in their rejection. Jesus warned Israel in Matthew 23:39, they would not see Him again until they acknowledged Him as their Messiah." [3]

Joel writes about this day when the nations gather. Just before the end of the Tribulation, Jesus will rescue Israel who is besieged by a multitude of nations whom He annihilates. At this time He will fulfill His most important promises to the Jews and bring them all (the remnant) to faith in Him (en masse).

ABOVE THE TRIBULATION

"Joel pictures Israel's heart of preparation for the Messiah over 600 years before the birth of Christ." [4]

> Blow the trumpet in Zion; consecrate a fast; call a solemn assembly; gather the people. Consecrate the congregation; assemble the elders; gather the children, even nursing infants. Let the bridegroom leave his room, and the bride her chamber. (Joel 2:15–16)

> You shall know that I am in the midst of Israel, and that I am the LORD your God and there is none else. And my people shall never again be put to shame. (Joel 2:27)

> On that day there shall be a fountain opened for the house of David and the inhabitants of Jerusalem, to cleanse them from sin and uncleanness. (Zec. 13:1)

> This is the new covenant I will make with the people of Israel on that day, says the Lord: I will put my laws in their minds, and I will write them on their hearts …. (Heb. 8:10 NLT)

Note however, that the Israelis (and the Jewish worldwide) will have suffered immeasurably prior to the Lord's rescue.

> In the whole land, declares the LORD, two thirds shall be cut off and perish, and one third shall be left alive. And I will put this third into the fire, and refine them as one refines silver, and test them as gold is tested. <u>They will call upon my name, and I will answer them.</u> I will say, "They are my people," and they will say, "The LORD is my God." (Zec. 13:8–9)

CHRIST'S VICTORY

Once the marriage *week* is complete, Jesus will thrill His Bride by allowing *her* to accompany Him on white horses as He descends upon earth to defeat the armies arrayed against Israel. (cf. Rev. 19:14) These victorious actions will culminate in His capture of Satan, Anti-Christ and False Prophet and throwing the latter two into the lake of fire and chaining Satan in the pit! (cf. Rev. 20:1–3)

Every person who is part of the Bride of Christ will have experienced (to one degree or another) the effects of Satan's monstrous deeds. So I do not believe it is a stretch to imagine their marveling at their *new Groom's* activities. To them, He will not only be King of Kings but also *Hero of Heroes.* (cf. 2 The. 1:10)

Christ's Bride will accompany Him when Jesus descends and defeats Satan (cf. Zec. 14:5, 1The. 3:13, Jude 14). "Revelation 17:14 speaks of those with the Lord at His coming as being 'called, chosen, and faithful,' all terms for believers (see Rom. 1:7, Eph. 1:1, 1Pet. 2:9)" [5] We will only be part of The Lord's Army; angels will also accompany Him.

We will all be elated at seeing Jesus rescue the Israelis (all remaining in Israel), who were massively besieged and facing certain annihilation. What a privilege it will be to see the Israelis' incredulity and wonder at being rescued so *unexpectedly.* As they realize who their rescuer is and the enormity of their sin, they will all retreat to their homes and individually mourn. They will bemoan their centuries of spiritual blindness (and resultant immeasurable suffering and terror) after having rejected their Messiah.

> And I will pour out on the house of David and the inhabitants of Jerusalem a spirit of grace and pleas for mercy, so that, when they look on me, on him whom they have pierced, they shall mourn for him, as one mourns for an only child, and weep bitterly over him, as one weeps over a firstborn. On that day the mourning in Jerusalem will be as great as the mourning for Hadad-rimmon in the

plain of Megiddo. The land shall mourn, each family by itself ... (Zec. 12:10–12a)

NOTE: One important fact that is overlooked by most is that not all Jews rejected Jesus (at His first advent). During the first ten years after Christ's resurrection, most converts to Christianity were Jews and their numbers were great. For example: after Peter's first sermon:

> And with many other words he bore witness and continued to exhort them, saying, "Save yourselves from this crooked generation." So those who received his word were baptized, and there were added that day about three thousand souls. (Acts. 2:40–41)

> And the Lord added to their number day by day those who were being saved. (Acts. 2:47)

So I would venture to say there were tens of thousands who followed Christ in just those first ten years (cf. Acts 21:20). That is probably why the Pharisees and in particular, Saul of Tarsus, were so desperate to *shut them down*.

A PROPHESIED GENTILE RESCUE

When Jesus rescues Israel and bestows salvation upon each Jew, He also *confers* salvation upon a remnant of Jerusalem's attackers and various other Gentiles. What an astonishing act of mercy at the climax of The Tribulation. This phenomenon is strongly implied in the following verse.

> Then it will come about that any who are left of all the nations that went against Jerusalem will go up from year to year to worship the King, the Lord of hosts, and to celebrate the Feast of Booths. (Zec. 14:16. NASB)

BEYOND THE RAPTURE

Here is the same verse in another translation:

> In the end, the enemies of Jerusalem who survive the plague will go up to Jerusalem each year to worship the King, the Lord of Heaven's Armies, and to celebrate the Festival of Shelters. (Zec. 14:16. NLT)

My first encounter with this verse sent me scrambling for the commentaries. I read a number of them. The majority of them concur that certain peoples, who are not destroyed by Jesus' plague, will either see (or hear of) Christ's victory, *come to their senses* and ask God to save them.

"Warned by these manifestations of God's power, the residue of the heathen shall be converted, and shall join with the Hebrews in the regular worship of Jehovah." [6]

As I pondered this mysterious passage, another set of verses came to mind. I am alluding to that time when Jesus will separate the sheep from the goats (cf. Mat. 25:37-46)

> "Then the righteous will answer Him, 'Lord, when did we see You hungry, and feed You, or thirsty, and give You something to drink? 'And when did we see You a stranger, and invite You in, or naked, and clothe You? 'When did we see You sick, or in prison, and come to You?' "The King will answer and say to them, 'Truly I say to you, to the extent that you did it to one of these brothers of Mine, even the least of them, you did it to Me.' (Mat. 25:37-40). NASB)

This unique and enigmatic set of verses precede the *sheep/goat* judgment and fit well with the thoughts about the Gentiles being saved (as indicated in Zechariah 14:16).

NATIONS AND ANGELS JUDGED

After Jesus rescues Israel, He next separates the goats

and the sheep. He gathers the nations and the angels (who rebelled) to be judged. In some mysterious way, we will be involved in this judgment.

> Do you not know that we are to judge angels? (1 Cor. 6:3)

"These are the angels who rebelled with Satan, and tempted and possessed humanity since the fall. This is one of the rewards Jesus will give to his faithful who bear his authority in the earth." [7]

"There will be a transition to the Kingdom of Messiah as nations will be judged for their actions during the Tribulation period. Some nations will not enter the Messianic Kingdom others will. Nations will be judged on how they treated the saints and/or the Jews during this period."[8]

NOTE: The entry of whole nations into the Millennium is a complicated topic because the ungodly will not be permitted to enter. I delve into this topic more thoroughly in Appendix H, Theoretical Governmental Model.

"This judgment is for those who are alive at the return of Christ. Those who died without Christ are not part of this judgment. This judgment is to determine who will enter the millennial kingdom of Messiah."[9]

> When the Son of Man comes in his glory, and all the angels with him, then he will sit on his glorious throne. Before him will be gathered all the nations, and he will separate people one from another as a shepherd separates the sheep from the goats. (Mat. 25:31–32)

At the end of the Great Tribulation, I believe Jesus will gather His Tribulation saints (those who are still alive) plus animal life and cocoon them until the wicked are taken away and the earth is repaired. Although this is not stated in Scripture, I feel this necessary due to the amount of devastation God unleashes on planet earth and our solar system.

ANTICHRIST'S AND FALSE PROPHET'S FATE

"The Beast and false prophet will be the first occupants of the Lake of Fire. The Lake of Fire will be the permanent dwelling of those who dwell in Hell. ... In the Lake of Fire they will be fully cognizant and aware of their fate." [10]

> And the beast was captured, and with it the false prophet who in its presence had done the signs by which he deceived those who had received the mark of the beast and those who worshiped its image. These two were thrown alive into the lake of fire that burns with sulfur. (Rev. 19:20)

SATAN BOUND FOR 1000 YEARS

> Then I saw an angel coming down from Heaven, holding in his hand the key to the bottomless pit and a great chain. And he seized the dragon, that ancient serpent, who is the devil and Satan, and bound him for a thousand years, and threw him into the pit, and shut it and sealed it over him, so that he might not deceive the nations any longer, until the thousand years were ended. (Rev. 20:1-3)

"In Hell Satan will be mocked and ridiculed by those who were terrified by him." [11]

> Your pomp is brought down to Sheol, the sound of your harps; maggots are laid as a bed beneath you, and worms are your covers. (Isaiah 14:11)

> But you are brought down to Sheol, to the far reaches of the pit. Those who see you will stare at you and ponder

ABOVE THE TRIBULATION

over you: 'Is this the man who made the earth tremble, who shook kingdoms, who made the world like a desert and overthrew its cities, who did not let his prisoners go home?' (Isa. 14:15–17)

I realize that these verses seem to be relating to when Satan's is suffering in Hell. But it would seem to be more practical and likely (to me) that he is viewed in his pathetic state while he is bound during the Millennium.

Some of the reasons Satan is bound are as follows:

- Satan is stripped of his earthly kingdom so it can be reclaimed and redeemed for the reign of Christ.

- For righteousness to flourish, Satan must be absent. (cf. Luke 8:12)

At this same time, Satan's evil angels will be bound (cf. Rev. 20:1–3). I infer that his evil angels will be bound or thrown in the lake of fire. John MacArthur concurs with this in his Bible Commentary regarding Revelation 20:2. Some of the reasons for this are as follows:

- For Satan to be effectively bound, his angels must be bound,

- Jesus Christ will have absolute power during the Millennium; therefore, fallen angels could not be present

- Satan's world system must be destroyed and forgotten.

BEYOND THE RAPTURE

God's truths will then obliterate all remnants of the *LIE* (all that Satan was). Satan cannot impede the tremendous harvest of souls to come.

---

1 Elliot, James Personal Journal
2 Truthnet.org, End times, Armageddon and Christ's Return, 7. Armies of the Earth gather to Israel, web
3 *ibid*. 8. Israel calls out to Messiah.
4 *ibid,*
5 Nelson, New Illustrated Bible Commentary, Revelation 17:14
6 Pulpit Commentary, volume 9
7 Truthnet.org, End times, 11. The Return of Messiah, web
8 *ibid.*
9 *ibid.*
10 *ibid.*
11 ibid.

CHAPTER 2

MILLENNIUM BEGINNINGS

> The Ancient One, the Most High, came and judged in favor of his holy people. Then the time arrived for the holy people to take over the kingdom. (Dan. 7:22 NLT)

> Then the sovereignty, power, and greatness of all the kingdoms under Heaven will be given to the holy people of the Most High. His kingdom will last forever, and all rulers will serve and obey him. (Dan. 7:27 NLT)

We saw in the last chapter that the Tribulation comes to an end with the glorious return of Christ and His dramatic defeat of Satan and the Antichrist and all his forces. Now let us delve into the exciting events that occur as The Millennium begins.

MILLENNIUM DISCOURSE

During this era (the Millennium), I believe Jesus will honor His Bride (the church) in incredible ways.

> But, as it is written, "... no eye has seen, nor ear heard, nor the heart of man imagined, what God has prepared for those who love Him" (1 Cor. 2:9b)

> Then the righteous will shine like the sun in their Father's Kingdom. Anyone with ears to hear should listen and understand! (Mat. 13:43 NLT)

> Then the King will say to those on his right, "Come, you who are blessed by my Father, inherit the Kingdom prepared for you from the creation of the world." (Mat.25:34 NLT)

More than all other nations, God will honor the Jews

and the land of Israel. This is addressed in depth later.

First and foremost however, the primary purpose of the Millennium is that Christ Jesus is exalted, glorified and worshipped. This is true of the Tribulation, the Millennium and the eternity to follow. Regardless of all the topics covered herein, the overriding important focus is the enthronement, worship and reign of our Lord and Savior. Not enough attention can be given His deity, supremacy and marvelous love for His creation. Of course, each member of the Godhead will be exalted, glorified and worshipped in new and wondrous ways.

The chapter entitled Purpose and Benefits of the Millennium (in this book) contains twenty-three purposes for the Millennium. I list a few of them here for your consideration:

1. It will allow God to fulfill all of His covenants and promises to the Jewish people.
2. God the Father fulfills His promises to Jesus.
3. Progressive revelation will show that God's road to salvation is the only way; and that His overall plan of the age is perfect.
4. Christ prepares His earthly Kingdom to present to God the Father, at the conclusion of His reign.
5. Far more souls will be won to Christ.

JESUS INITIATES THE MILLENNIUM

"Undoubtedly the millennial kingdom will be a dispensation graphically different from any previous one and involving many unique features which can only

MILLENNIUM BEGINNINGS

partially be understood now from the Scriptures. As a dispensation it is fitted to be climactic in its character and a divine preparation for the eternal state." [1]

> God has made "known to us the mystery of his will, according to his purpose, which he set forth in Christ as a plan for the fullness of time, to unite all things in him, things in Heaven and things on earth." (Eph. 1:9, 10)

With the Antichrist and False Prophet cast into hell and Satan now bound for a thousand years, Christ begins to establish His millennial kingdom, starting with the judgment of the nations to remove all those who will not be permitted to enter into this kingdom of righteousness over which Jesus will rule. At the end of the Tribulation, Jesus' next major activity will be to repair and craft the millennial earth for habitation. He would also repair damage to sun, moon and our solar system. This is necessitated due to the destruction God unleashes during the Great Tribulation.

> I watched as the Lamb broke the sixth seal, and there was a great earthquake. The sun became as dark as black cloth, and the moon became as red as blood. Then the stars of the sky fell to the earth like green figs falling from a tree shaken by a strong wind. The sky was rolled up like a scroll, and all of the mountains and islands were moved from their places. (Rev. 6:12–14)

Other repair may be required due to the aftermath of nuclear warfare. We get just a hint of this type of activity from this verse:

> I will repopulate your cities, and the ruins will be rebuilt (Ezk.36:33c NLT)

Perhaps Jesus will employ the Millennial mortal Jews in a special way in the land of Israel. The prince of prophets, Isaiah, speaks of such action.

BEYOND THE RAPTURE

They will rebuild the ancient ruins, repairing cities destroyed long ago. They will revive them, though they have been deserted for many generations. (Isa. 61:4)

RESURRECTION OF OT SAINTS

The first of a number of important events will be the resurrection of the Old Testament (OT) Saints. Bible scholars believe that OT saints (as well as Tribulation martyrs) will not be resurrected until Christ's Second Advent (His second coming to earth when He rescues Israel, which initiates the beginning of the Millennium – *see: Isaiah 26:19-21 and Daniel 12:1-2)*. The interesting aspect of this timing is how it fits perfectly into the *Marriage of the Lamb* scenario.

READINESS

In some special manner, Jesus will cause (or will have caused previously) the OT Saints to understand what He had accomplished during their absence:

- His incarnation
- His Messianic Ministry
- His sacrificial death on the cross
- His resurrection
- The ministry of the Holy Spirit
- The ministry of His Holy Apostles
- The infolding of the Gentiles
- The Church Age

MILLENNIUM BEGINNINGS

- The Rapture
- The Tribulation

Jesus may cluster the OT saints who comprise Christ's wedding party apart from the Tribulation survivors in preparation for the arrival and presentation of His Bride.

How exactly Jesus preserves Tribulation survivors during His reconstruction of the Heavens and Earth is not specified in the Bible. But once the earth is ready, they would be reintroduced to it. The most eminent of them would be the 144,000 of the twelve tribes of Israel who evangelized Earth's citizenry during The Tribulation. I believe that Jesus will gather all of the Tribulation Survivor saints within (or near) Israel. He will do this in preparation for several important events.

WEDDING SUPPER OF THE LAMB

And the angel said to me, "Write this: Blessed are those who are invited to the marriage supper of the Lamb." And he said to me, "These are the true words of God." (Rev. 19:9)

One of the greatest events of all church history will be the celebration of the Wedding Supper of the Lamb. This incredible event is based on ancient Jewish tradition. It is marvelous to see how Christ fulfills this. Briefly, it is the "wedding banquet held after a one-week cloistered honeymoon." *To understand this better, please reference Appendix E, "Ancient Jewish Wedding Practices."* Jesus may orchestrate His Wedding Supper as follows:

The wedding supper attendants would be certain OT saints. The guests will include all OT saints and mortal

Jews but not Gentiles (according to some experts). However, John MacArthur states the following: "These are those who were saved before Pentecost ... the guests will also include tribulation saints and believers alive in earthly bodies in the kingdom." ²

Many of the notables of the Bible would undoubtedly play significant roles in this ceremony. I definitely believe that one prominent figure would be Abraham. He is the father of the children of promise (that is, all who belong to God by faith).

> In the same way, "Abraham believed God, and God counted him as righteous because of his faith." The real children of Abraham, then, are those who put their faith in God. What's more, the Scriptures looked forward to this time when God would declare the Gentiles to be righteous because of their faith. God proclaimed this good news to Abraham long ago when he said, "All nations will be blessed through you." So all who put their faith in Christ share the same blessing Abraham received because of his faith. (Gal.3:6–9 NLT)

So Abraham, Sarah and other notables would be escorted into the Wedding Banquet hall. This could possibly be in the New Jerusalem; and if so Abraham might feel blessed even more than others. Consider the following verse:

> Abraham was confidently looking forward to a city with eternal foundations, a city designed and built by God (Heb. 11:10 NLT)

This OT entourage would be introduced to the Bride of Christ. Great excitement and celebration would follow as they are introduced to one another. This would be Jesus' grand reception celebrating His marriage to His Bride (the

MILLENNIUM BEGINNINGS

New Testament [NT] Church).

This interpretation of the Wedding Supper is somewhat speculative due to the uncertainty of Bible scholars regarding this topic. Some regard the entire Millennium as the Wedding Supper. This is based on applying the parable about the king's wedding (Matthew 22:1-14 and Luke 14:15–24) to the Tribulation and Millennium. Some view the Tribulation as a time when again the Jews are invited to the King's Son's wedding. This will be followed by the rescued Jews attending this wedding at the beginning of (and perhaps throughout) the Millennium. Although we get an inkling of what will be taking place, there remains considerable mystery.

THE CORONATION OF CHRIST

The Coronation of Christ could be the first event which will happen once mortals and animals have been established in Christ's new kingdom (cf. "Animals Section" in Chapter 8, Kingdom Details for further detail).

> God has highly exalted him and bestowed on him the name that is above every name, so that at the name of Jesus every knee should bow, in Heaven and on earth and under the earth, and every tongue confess that Jesus Christ is Lord, to the glory of God the Father. (Php. 2:8–11)

In my opinion, His Coronation will be the most important event to ever happen in our universe. In the greater sense, Jesus' coronation is unnecessary. He is already enthroned at the right hand of God. But perhaps, His coronation would be important in the same way as when Jesus asked John to baptize Him. When John said in effect, "No Lord, you should baptize me!" Jesus responded:

"It should be done, for we must carry out all that God requires." So John agreed to baptize him. After his baptism, as Jesus came up out of the water, the heavens were opened and he saw the Spirit of God descending like a dove and settling on him. (Mat. 3:15b–16 NLT)

So the Coronation of Christ Jesus will occur in the presence of all the new inhabitants of the Millennial Earth, so they can experience His enthronement as their God and reigning monarch (of not just earth but of all creation).

His Bride, Old Testament Saints, the Tribulation Martyred Saints, and mortal saints might celebrate this event for months. Days of worship would surround the Coronation.

Worship will be beyond our comprehension in terms of exultation in joy. The coronation, itself, might begin with a procession through and among all mortals. Recall Jesus' Triumphant Entry into Jerusalem (during His first advent, cf. Mat. 21:1–11). Old Testament Saints, angels and godly creatures (for example: the four living creatures covered with eyes – Revelation 4:6) will all be present. The angels, themselves, would be a spectacle. We get an idea of the wonder they would invoke from the following passages which illustrates the splendor of angels:

> I, John, am the one who heard and saw these things. And when I heard and saw them, I fell down to worship at the feet of the angel who showed them to me. (Rev. 22:8)

> I lifted up my eyes and looked, and behold, a man clothed in linen, with a belt of fine gold from Uphaz around his waist. His body was like beryl, his face like the appearance of lightning, his eyes like flaming torches, his arms and legs like the gleam of burnished bronze, and the sound of his words like the sound of a multitude. (Dan. 10:5–6)

MILLENNIUM BEGINNINGS

In one possible scenario, Jesus would be borne on His Throne by Cherubim (Ezekiel 10). In another scenario Jesus might ride in a beautifully adorned carriage pulled by white horses. A colt (symbolic of the colt He rode into Jerusalem) might walk behind His carriage. Another possibility is that Jesus would ride a magnificent white horse (as mentioned in Tribulation Events).

His processional road could be of smooth sapphire (translucent, lapis-colored [cf. Exo. 24:10]) and strewn with appropriate flowers, streamers, carpets, leaves and the like. The Holy Spirit may have commissioned and empowered certain beings to plan, design and supervise the entire coronation event (cf. Exo. 31:1–6).

Seraphim would fly above and around His entourage singing and uttering praises. (Ala Isaiah 6:1–3) Jesus, Himself, will be spectacular in appearance. Though He came to earth in the form of a common person without any attractive physical features (Isaiah 53:2), He will now reveal Himself in glory and majesty.

> And in the midst of the lampstands one like a son of man, clothed with a long robe and with a golden sash around his chest. The hairs of his head were white, like white wool, like snow. His eyes were like a flame of fire, his feet were like burnished bronze, refined in a furnace, and his voice was like the roar of many waters. In his right hand he held seven stars, from his mouth came a sharp two-edged sword, and his face was like the sun shining in full strength. (Rev. 1:13–16)

I believe that when Jesus reveals Himself, He will not appear so formidable but more human-like with His kind, loving spirit manifested.

Choirs could be at strategic places joining the Seraphim

in grand choral song (cf. Rev. 5:9). All He passes would exult and yet weep with joy, as they prostrated themselves in worship. The procession would proceed to Jerusalem where His Throne (a representation of God's throne in Heaven) would await Him. No doubt a rainbow would encircle Him (cf. Rev. 4:3).

> I heard a sound from Heaven like the roar of mighty ocean waves or the rolling of loud thunder. It was like the sound of many harpists playing together. This great choir sang a wonderful new song in front of the throne of God and before the four living beings and the twenty-four elders. (Rev. 14:2–3 NLT)

Once Jesus arrived, He could choose to reveal His Bride and do so in spectacular fashion. He would raise His hands and call for *her*. All eyes would turn heavenward expectantly.

> I saw the holy city, New Jerusalem, coming down out of Heaven from God, prepared as a bride adorned for her husband. (Rev. 21:2)

NOTE: Although this mention of New Jerusalem follows the Great White Throne Judgment, its description is consistent with its appearance at the beginning of the Millennium as mentioned by John when the angel reveals New Jerusalem as the Bride of Christ in verses 21:9b–10.

Once the magnificent eternal city descends to a certain height, a veritable cloud of Bride Saints will descend upon the area and take their place to honor their King. Representatives of His Bride (perhaps the Apostles [cf. Rev. 5:1–10]) could stand beside Him. The resurrected John, the Baptist (and/or Elijah), might speak the words leading to His enthronement and then God the Father might speak a wonderful message and declare Him Lord of our universe. The Holy Spirit could make His appearance in the form of a magnificent Dove and alight on Jesus' shoulder (cf. Mat. 3:16). Jesus could then receive His scepter and God place an ethereal crown upon His head.

> And to him was given dominion and glory and a kingdom, that all peoples, nations, and languages should serve him; his dominion is an everlasting dominion, which shall not pass away, and his kingdom one that shall not be destroyed (Dan. 7:14)

> And the twenty-four elders, who were seated on their thrones before God, fell on their faces and worshiped God, saying:
> "We give thanks to you, Lord God Almighty,
> the One who is and who was,
> because you have taken your great power
> and have begun to reign. (Rev. 11:16-17 NIV)

The words of Isaiah also seem appropriate here:

> I saw the Lord, high and exalted, seated on a throne; and the train of his robe filled the temple. Above him were seraphim, each with six wings: With two wings they covered their faces, with two they covered their feet, and with two they were flying. And they were calling to one another:
> "Holy, holy, holy is the Lord Almighty;
> the whole earth is full of his glory." (Isa. 6:1a–4 NIV)

Christ's glorification might momentarily diminish as Jesus next speaks wondrous words to all His subjects. Every part of the ceremony could be interspersed with songs from choirs of angels and godly beings. (cf. Mat 3:16)

Lest I trivialize this event in any way, realize that the ideas just posited must somehow be reconciled with God's majestic glory as portrayed in the following scene in

BEYOND THE RAPTURE

Heaven.

> Behold, a throne stood in Heaven, with one seated on the throne. And he who sat there had the appearance of jasper and carnelian, and around the throne was a rainbow that had the appearance of an emerald. Around the throne were twenty-four thrones, and seated on the thrones were twenty-four elders, clothed in white garments, with golden crowns on their heads. From the throne came flashes of lightning, and rumblings and peals of thunder, and before the throne were burning seven torches of fire, which are the seven spirits of God, and before the throne there was as it were a sea of glass, like crystal.
>
> And around the throne, on each side of the throne, are four living creatures, full of eyes in front and behind: the first living creature like a lion, the second living creature like an ox, the third living creature with the face of a man, and the fourth living creature like an eagle in flight. And the four living creatures, each of them with six wings, are full of eyes all around and within, and day and night they never cease to say, Holy, holy, holy, is the Lord God Almighty, who was and is and is to come! (Rev. 4:2b–8)

The song, *I Can Only Imagine*, as performed by Mercy Me (on YouTube) rather captures the emotions we might be feeling as we experience all this: Another performance we really enjoyed is 8-year old Rhema Maryanne's song, *No More Night*. www.godvine.com

INTRODUCTION OF THE BRIDE

At the conclusion of the ceremony, Jesus could invite all in attendance to meet His Bride. The following verse might describe how Jesus will treat people at this event (an extension of the marriage supper of the lamb):

> In Jerusalem, the Lord of Heaven's Armies will spread a wonderful feast for all the people of the world. It will be a

MILLENNIUM BEGINNINGS

delicious banquet with clear, well-aged wine and choice meat. (Isa. 25:6 NLT)

There will probably be a huge celebration lasting weeks as Jesus reveals His creation to His Bride (that is, His Temple, the resplendent earthly Jerusalem, Israel and glorious earth beyond, freed from the curse). Jesus may also introduce His Bride to His Father and the Holy Spirit (officially) apart from mortals (and maybe from OT saints).

Being God, Jesus will be able to sustain this bridal relationship with millions and even billions of saints. At the same time all of us in this relationship will be completely knowing and loving of one another and this too, eternally.

In addition to this, we will probably have a more personal relationship with God the Father – getting acquainted with His personage. Mortal humans were never able to see God the Father or the Holy Spirit (cf. John 1:18). When on earth we only knew The Father vicariously through Jesus, the Holy Spirit and The Word. But it seems logical that in our immortal bodies as the Bride of Christ, we will personally experience our magnificent Father God.

On earth, the Holy Spirit (the third member of the Triune Godhead) was our Guide, Teacher and Counselor who always interceded on our behalf. I would suggest that He would continue as *God, our best friend.* He could help us be all we should be as Bride of Christ, Children of God the Father and co-regents with them in the Millennial Age. Perhaps you struggle with my calling the Holy Spirit *best friend* but really is He not our constant companion now? Currently He facilitates the presence of God the Father and Jesus within us. He guides us into all truth (cf. John 14:23).

Another celebration will *rival* that of the *Bride of*

BEYOND THE RAPTURE

Christ's. In many Scriptures, God refers to Israel as His bride (c.f.. Hosea 2:19, 20). A pastor at a church we attended explained that Christians are Christ's heavenly bride whereas Israel is God's earthly bride. This is a mystery to me yet it is a stated phenomenon.

The phenomenon that immortals and angels will observe with ecstasy will be Jesus' dynamic revelation of His loving plan for the glorification of Israel with Jerusalem its focus. Concurrent with that will be Israeli's increasing incredulity as Jesus showers them with godly love and attention. Each will praise God again and again as they become the envy of people worldwide. There will undoubtedly be many a celebration throughout the nation of Israel feting their reunion with God.

Israel will also exult in their newfound peace and magnificent nation. God will have expanded her tenfold in fulfillment of prophecy (cf. Isa. 26:15, 33:17, Oba. 17–21, Mic. 7:14). "The expanded Israel will encompass half of Egypt, all of Lebanon, Jordan, Syria, and Kuwait plus three fourths of Iraq and Saudi Arabia." [3]

---

1 Walvoord, John, *The Millennial Kingdom*, 330

2. MacArthur, John, *MacArthur Bible Commentary*, Rev. 19:9

3. DeYoung. Jimmy, ProphecyToday.org, Weekly Podcast 012, web

CHAPTER 3

THE NEW JERUSALEM

Once the wedding celebration is concluded, Jesus could then proceed in setting up His Kingdom. Jerusalem (as well as the newly expanded Israel) will be recreated in total magnificence. *This will be discussed in greater detail in Chapter 4, The Kingdom, Millennial Jerusalem.*

Before considering Christ's Kingdom, let us give thought to our heavenly home. As I mentioned before, most scholars of a pretribulational view believe the New Jerusalem will be the home of Christ's Bride (as well of all other immortals).

So let us consider some of the qualities of this spectacular supernatural city. Some believe that the New Jerusalem will hover above Israel. Because of its size (a spectacular *cube* 1400 miles per *side*,) it may orbit earth like our moon.

> He showed me the holy city, Jerusalem, descending out of Heaven from God. It shone with the glory of God and sparkled like a precious stone – like jasper as clear as crystal. The city wall was road and high, with twelve gates guarded by twelve angels. And the names of the twelve tribes of Israel were written on the gates. There were three gates on each side – east, north, south, and west. The wall of the city had twelve foundation stones, and on them were written the names of the twelve apostles of the Lamb. (Rev 21:10b–14 NLT)

It is the general opinion of biblical scholars that the Bride of Christ, OT saints, Tribulation martyred saints and angels will live with Jesus and God in the New Jerusalem during the Millennium (this issue is addressed in greater depth later).

> But you have come to Mount Zion and to the city of the living God, the heavenly Jerusalem, and to innumerable angels in festal gathering, and to the assembly of the firstborn who are enrolled in Heaven, and to God, the judge of all, and to the spirits of the righteous made perfect, and to Jesus, the mediator of a new covenant ,,,. (Heb. 12:22-24b)

In the Hebrews *Hall of Faith*, it says the following:

> These all died in faith, not having received the things promised, but having seen them and greeted them from afar, and having acknowledged that they were strangers and exiles on the earth ... But as it is, they desire a better country, that is, a heavenly one. Therefore God is not ashamed to be called their God, for he has prepared for them a city. (Heb. 11:13, 16)

OUR HEAVENLY HOME

When my wife and I went on our first cruise, we sailed *The Vision of the Seas* (Royal Caribbean). Its main restaurant was spectacular. There were *outside* elevators at one end which were resplendent. There were beautiful *floating* winding stairs in the middle. It was breathtaking and my first thought was, "This is what the New Jerusalem will be like."

Imagine the most wonderful, luxurious accommodations you have ever seen. I am certain Jesus will create each of our heavenly homes to be vastly superior to that luxury. I expect them to have a regal beauty comparable to New Jerusalem's exterior. *I deduce this from*

THE NEW JERUSALEM

Isaiah 54:11-12. Jesus has prepared us a home of such magnificence that each of us will gasp at its splendor.

Considering that he knows each of us personally, I believe He will craft a residence for each that will reflect all that person enjoys and holds dear in this world. For example: If a person enjoys flowers, his home would be replete with plants bearing incredibly spectacular flowers. Such a setting would probably be completed with butterflies and song birds. Whatever (and however many) facets of God's creation a Christian enjoyed on earth will somehow be incorporated into his heavenly domicile.

Jesus knows and loves each of us personally; therefore I would expect He will create an individualized home for each Christian so as to show His affection and kindness to each of us. But I believe that we will have continual access to the Lord; He will commune with each of us in our own home (as well as anywhere else we go in the universe).

Furthermore, our heavenly home will in no way be isolated. Each will be part of a *village* of those dearest to its occupant. Do you like to party? We will party! It will be part worship, part celebration, part entertainment and meaningful fun. God will provide the means as well as facilitate the activities.

Recall that Jesus said, "Blessed are you who weep now, for you will laugh." (Luke 6:21) He also said, "There is rejoicing in the presence of the angels of God over one sinner who repents." (Luke 15:10 NLT) Laughter and rejoicing await us.

In John's Gospel, Jesus proclaims:

In My Father's house there are many dwelling places (homes). If it were not so, I would have told you; for I am

BEYOND THE RAPTURE

going away to prepare a place for you. And when I go and make ready a place for you, I will come back again and will take you to Myself, that where I am you may be also. (John 14:2–3)

These verses are the basis for my conjecture. However for me, the most significant promise is "I . . . will take you to Myself, that where I am you may be also…"

LIFE IN NEW JERUSALEM

The aura within New Jerusalem will be extraordinary. Please allow me to present some possibilities:

Jesus will have adorned the interior with amazingly beautiful décor and rolling landscapes with winding paths lined with beautiful flowers.

Enchanting music invoking worship could waft across the scene. As one gazed toward things distant, dancing swirling colors reminiscent of the aurora borealis would enhance each scene. Some homes could resemble the thatched cottages that dot the English countryside (especially in the Cotswolds). Every home would appear warm and welcoming. Wonderful favorite fragrances would permeate the air. As we Bride Saints bathe ourselves in this marvelous ambience, we would be experiencing wonderful connectivity with our Lord. Everyone we encounter would provide instantaneous warm friendship. We will be fascinated with one another, always loving, gracious and engaging.

Angels may drift about doing such things as greeting us, meeting needs, or sharing information. They might introduce us to others the Lord wants us to meet or update us about the exciting events on earth. They could bid us

THE NEW JERUSALEM

come directly into God's presence. At other times, they might take us to a situation in which one of our mortal acquaintances (or relatives) is about to accept Christ; and then on to the angelic celebration about their having done so. Angels could summon us to an assignment God has for us or invite us to a special time of worship. At other times, they could direct us to various celebrations or parties. Another of their assignments could be to invite us to an audience with an OT or NT notable.

Regardless of what we might do by way of entertainment or activities, we would always be returning to Christ Jesus, adoring Him, dwelling on His every Word, gazing into His eyes increasingly more incredulous at the position, glory and attention He showers upon us in love.

NEW JERUSALEM'S EXTERIOR

It shone with the glory of God and sparkled like a precious stone – like jasper as clear as crystal. (Rev. 21:11)

The twelve tribes of Judah have their names inscribed on the gates and the twelve Apostles' names are on the foundation stones (cf. Rev.21:12–14). These stones remind us that the Apostles' work and writings formed the foundation for the church. The names of the tribes of Israel underscore that through Israel, God provided out Savior, our Bible, covenants and promises (cf. Rom. 9:4-5).

The foundations of the Holy City are inlaid with the twelve precious stones that represent Israel. These same stones were found on the breast plate of the OT priests' vestments. Each stone represented a tribe and those twelve stones were arrayed in the same order as the tribes encamped around the Tabernacle in the wilderness.

Each of those twelve immense gates is one huge pearl. Various artists have endeavored to portray the exterior of this city, but I cannot believe any came close to the splendor of God's masterful creation. The cover of the predecessor to this book, *Christ's Spectacular Millennium,* only hints at what might be – what is shown is part of a famous *huge* diamond (representing the New Jerusalem).

One might ask, "If the Bride of Christ is the primary group of occupants, why is the exterior of New Jerusalem so laden with Jewish symbolism?" The answer is found in Romans 11:11–26 in which the Gentiles are deemed *ingrafted* into the olive tree (which is Israel). Remember, the Apostle Paul emphasized the concept "to the Jew first and also to the Greek," (cf. Rom. 1:16). Our gracious God is committed to honoring and restoring Israel. His Old Testament saints will reside in New Jerusalem as well as the Bride of Christ. How or if God will include the Millennial Jews in the eternal city is not known.

One thing to note is the extensive use of the number 12: 12 angels, 12 gates, 12 foundation stones, 12 apostles, 12 tribes of Israel, and 12 gems. Twelve is often the number representing government in the Bible.

NEW JERUSALEM'S INTERIOR

The internal design of New Jerusalem is left to our imagination. I suspect that it will not have floors and rooms (or suites) like a skyscraper or condo. Rather, I think it will be multi-dimensional with mansions and their estates *floating* at various levels and placements. Somehow the

THE NEW JERUSALEM

streets of gold could form curving spirals winding from one beautiful home to the next. The gold of the streets is translucent (some say it is not only translucent but also iridescent).

What can we infer from what is said about New Jerusalem? For one, it is a city; that implies community, togetherness. It is a God-sustained, *self-sufficient* entity where we will exist with our God, totally and completely joyous and content. It is an eternal and magnificently-crafted world given to us by our God. It is huge and its overall dimension emphasizes our ability to traverse its expanse with ease. It is glorious and magnifies our God. Because of its magnificence, we will never cease to revel in its (and therefore God's) beauty. All we experience there will speak of Christ's love for us. Our complete fellowship with all three members of the Godhead, the angels and one another will reverberate with fulfillment and pleasure. Yet all I have said is complete understatement!

NEW JERUSALEM CONTROVERSY

Before discussing New Jerusalem's location, let me clarify the timing of New Jerusalem's appearances. It is described as coming down out of Heaven in two instances in Revelation 21. In the first verse, the New Jerusalem comes down to earth after the New Earth is created (cf. Rev. 21:2). This follows the description of (and is clearly after) the Great White Throne Judgment (cf. Rev. 20:11–15)

The second mention of the New Jerusalem (cf. Rev. 21:9) however, is determined to be at the beginning of the Millennium. It is confusing because of the order of the two descriptions of New Jerusalem's descent. Whereas, Revelation 21:1-8, is about the New Heaven and Earth, Revelation 21:9-22:7 describes events in the Millennium.

"The view held by Darby, Gaebelein, Grant, Ironside, Jennings, Kelly, Pettingill, Seiss, Scott and others is the view that after describing the eternal state in Revelation 21:1-8 John gives a recapitulation of the millennial age, in order to describe more fully that period of time."[1]

Walvoord agrees with this assessment: "It may be demonstrated from Scripture ... the heavenly Jerusalem is in existence in the Millennium." [2]

This information was most helpful to me just to understand apparent contradictions in Revelation 21:27 and 22:15. These similar verses simply cannot pertain to the time of the New Heaven and New Earth in which there is no unrighteousness. For example, examine the following verses:

> All the nations will bring their glory and honor into the city. Nothing evil will be allowed to enter, nor anyone who practices shameful idolatry and dishonesty – but only those whose names are written in the Lamb's Book of Life. (Rev. 21:26-28 NLT)

NEW JERUSALEM'S LOCATION

The angel who talked to me held in his hand a gold measuring stick to measure the city, its gates, and its wall. When he measured it, he found it was a square, as wide as it was long. In fact, its length and width and height were each 1,400 miles. (Rev. 21:15-16)

A city of 1,960,000 square miles cannot *sit* on Israel (by

human reckoning). First of all, the dimensions far exceed the newly expanded Israel (as prophesied). Currently Israel is approximately 8,000 square miles. In the Millennium, it is projected to be <u>80,000</u> square miles (by virtue of what God allotted her in the Old Testament). Since the base of New Jerusalem is nearly <u>two million</u> square miles, Bible analysts feel it must float above earth in some manner. Visitors to the Holy City would have to be ferried by some God-provided conveyance.

It is generally agreed by interpreters ... that the city seen in Revelation 21:10 is suspended over the earth.[3]

This magnificent palatial creation from God is designated The Holy City. However, just the bottom *floor* is larger than many countries, for example: it is half the size of continental USA. Because it rises to a height of 1400 miles and is to be evidently occupied from top to bottom, it really takes on the qualities of a unique planet. Its overall presence will be miraculous to all. God will employ special measures to sustain a *hollow* entity this large. Since Jesus sustains our entire universe (cf. Heb. 1:3), this will be a small matter to Him. We might very well dub New Jerusalem, the *God Planet.* I await seeing Christ's spectacular home for us with excitement and great anticipation.

Since the city probably does not come down completely, two possibilities come to mind. The city could hover high above earthly Jerusalem itself or it could orbit the earth as a spectacular moon. I believe moon (or satellite) is a better choice simply because of New Jerusalem's size and what would seem to be the advantages of orbiting God's *Blue Planet.*

BEYOND THE RAPTURE

Our moon is approximately 2160 miles in diameter, whereas, the New Jerusalem is a 1400 mile (per side) cube with a 2.74 billion cubic miles volume, (about half the volume of the moon). Because the New Jerusalem will be an immense, spectacular *palace*, we are comparing two different entities.

If we compared habitable areas, the New Jerusalem has an astoundingly greater capacity than the earth and the moon combined. The total land area of earth is 57.5 million square miles. If Jesus put one *floor* every 30 vertical feet of the New Jerusalem, there would be 493 billion square miles of *housing* area. As you can see, the habitable area eclipses that of earth astronomically and ridiculously so, the surface area of the moon (14.7 million square miles).

"Expositors differ as to whether the city is in the form of a cube or a pyramid."[4]

Were New Jerusalem in a pyramid configuration, its *floor space* would be one third the volume of the cubed version or (using the model above) 164 billion square miles.

This is still three thousand times the *land* size of earth. I, myself, envision New Jerusalem as a multi-faceted, spheroid sparkling somewhat like a stunning, glittering multifaceted enormous diamond. I realize that is an anemic comparison But it might help make the point that New Jerusalem will be magnificent beyond our comprehension.

It does not appear that the moon will be replaced by the New Jerusalem. Several times in Ezekiel it mentions the *Festival of the New Moon* (re: Ezekiel 46:1, 66:2). Will God orchestrate two *moons* for planet earth? Whether New

THE NEW JERUSALEM

Jerusalem will remain in geosynchronous orbit over Israel or orbit the earth, God's city will be spectacular and will be seen consistently by most of earth's inhabitants.

In some way New Jerusalem will provide light to earth's inhabitants (and of course God is the source of New Jerusalem's light). How this is orchestrated is unknown. Whereas God's light continually bathes Jerusalem (cf. Isa. 60:19–20), there will be night and day over the rest of earth. (cf. Isa. 30:26).

OUR TRAVELS

Whatever the case, we will be dwelling in the eternal city, New Jerusalem. The incredible size of its interior suggests that we will be able to traverse its internal expanse supernaturally with ease. Now let us extrapolate a little. Since we will be living with God in His city, it would seem that we will *commute* to fulfill our responsibilities on earth. Since we will all have spiritual bodies, this will probably be a *trivial matter*.

With such a scenario, *earthlings* may (or may not) be able to see (or sense) our *coming and going*. However it happens, earthlings will know of our abode and maybe our general movements. This would be but one contributing factor to their awe of Christ's Kingdom. As I think about it, I am reminded of *Jacob's ladder*.

1 Pentecost, J. Dwight *Things to Come*, 563
2 Walvoord, John, *The Millennial Kingdom*, 324
3 Pentecost, J. Dwight *ibid.*, 569
4 Walvoord, John, *ibid.* 334

CHAPTER 4

CHRIST'S KINGDOM

MILLENNIAL JERUSALEM

To establish the correct perspective of Christ's reign, we must begin with the ancient city of Jerusalem. It will become the most exalted city of the whole earth. Jesus will minister to all the Millennial inhabitants from there. Jerusalem's role and appearance will be magnificent. Jesus will have changed its very topography (cf. Zec. 14:2-5) to best display and support His temple and seat of government. This chapter will also consider how He establishes His Kingdom at the outset.

Jerusalem's primary feature will be Christ's temple. From it, He will reign both spiritually and governmentally. From it will issue the River of Healing. In it rulers and others will worship Christ (cf. Zec. 14:9, 17, Psa. 47:7-9). All that is Jerusalem will focus on Jesus, honoring Him and revering Him; and it will be a wonderful privilege for mortal Israelis to live there.

Currently, Jerusalem is of great significance to four major religions: Judaism, Islam, Roman Catholicism and orthodox Christianity. By contrast, Christ's all-encompassing monarchy, His Temple and the River of Life will be the only and all-sufficient focus in Jerusalem during the Millennium.

> This is what the Lord of Heaven's Armies says: "My love for Mount Zion is passionate and strong; I am consumed with passion for Jerusalem!"

BEYOND THE RAPTURE

> And now the Lord says: I am returning to Mount Zion, and I will live in Jerusalem. Then Jerusalem will be called the Faithful City; the mountain of the Lord of Heaven's Armies will be called the Holy Mountain. (Zec. 8:2–3 NLT)

> Shout, and sing for joy, O inhabitant of Zion, for great in your midst is the Holy One of Israel. (Isa. 12:6)

> For the Lord's teaching will go out from Zion; his word will go out from Jerusalem. (Mic. 4:2e)

As you can deduce, since Jesus reigns over a worldwide monarchy from Jerusalem, it will be the center of the earth. She will be its very capital (spiritually and governmentally). All life will flow from Christ (and therefore Jerusalem) spiritually as well as physically.

Jesus will cause her to be resplendent, echoing God's glory. Isaiah describes just how spectacularly our Lord will transform her.

> I will rebuild you with precious jewels
>   and make your foundations from lapis lazuli.
> I will make your towers of sparkling rubies,
>   your gates of shining gems,
>   and your walls of precious stones. (Isa. 54:11b–12.NLT)

He will make His presence ever-manifest by His Shekinah Glory. It will be visible over the city, a cloud by day and a fire by night.

> Rise from the dust, O Jerusalem. Sit in a place of honor. (Isa. 52:2a).

> Wake up, wake up, O Zion! Clothe yourself with strength. Put on your beautiful clothes, O holy city of Jerusalem, (Isa. 52:1a)

> Then the Lord will provide shade for Mount Zion and all who assemble there. He will provide a canopy of

cloud during the day and smoke and flaming fire at night covering the glorious land. It will be a shelter from daytime heat and a hiding place from storms and rain. (Isa. 4:5–6)

These preceding verses just begin to describe Jerusalem's (and her people's) marvelous inheritance. You can obtain a better overall sense of how magnificently Jesus will endow her by reading all of Isaiah 60.

THE TEMPLE

One of Jesus' first actions in Jerusalem will be to build His temple. First He will supernaturally transform the temple mount into a grand mountain. (cf. Isa. 2.2) Atop this mount, He will create His magnificent temple as prophesied by the prophet, Ezekiel (Chapters 40–47). His temple (and its surrounds) will be spectacularly beautiful beyond comprehension. God's glory will emanate like a dazzling jewel for all to behold. It will tower over Jerusalem as God's banner over the entire world.

Merrill Unger lists and expands upon five purposes for the Millennial Temple:

1. "To demonstrate God's holiness

2. To provide a dwelling place for the Divine Glory.

3. To perpetuate the memorial of sacrifice.

4. To provide the centre for divine government.

5. To provide victory over the curse." [1]

NOTE: He also points out that the healing and life-giving waters issuing from the River of Life flowing from the temple) afford this victory.

BEYOND THE RAPTURE

As you and I consider the Millennial Temple, it seems both logical and wonderful that Jesus would build a temple from which to reign. We have little trouble accepting this scenario, either historically or spiritually. However, to the Jewish (whether they come from The Tribulation, are Messianic immortal Jews or OT saints,) the Temple, recreated by their Messiah, is fulfillment of a long-standing desire (both generational and communal)!

For millennia, Jews have mourned the loss and lack of a temple during Tisha B'Av. The non-coincidental destruction of both the Solomonic (586 BC) and Herodian (70 AD) temples occurred on the ninth of Av (Tisha B'Av). Furthermore, a number of other anti-Semitic catastrophes occurred on Tisha B'Av. Traditionally religious Jews hold that their disobedience caused God to consign them to wander in the desert for forty years on Tisha B'Av. So you can understand why to both the mortal and immortal Jews, Christ's Temple will be of immense significance and cause for celebration. As they *resume* worship in this temple, it will hold on-going importance in a multitude of ways.

As just mentioned, one of the unique features of the Millennial Temple is the River of Healing which flows from the threshold of its doors.

> Then he brought me back to the door of the temple, and behold, water was issuing from below the threshold of the temple toward the east (for the temple faced east). The water was flowing down from below the south end of the threshold of the temple, south of the altar. Then he brought me out by way of the north gate and led me around on the outside to the outer gate that faces toward the east; and behold, the water was trickling out on the south side. (Ezk. 47:1–2)

Ezekiel watches the man walk *down* the river. It

CHRIST'S KINGDOM

deepens from ankle depth to over his head within a mile. Some of the marvelous attributes of this river are as follows:

> He asked me, "Have you been watching, son of man?" Then he led me back along the riverbank. When I returned, I was surprised by the sight of many trees growing on both sides of the river. Then he said to me, "This river flows east through the desert into the valley of the Dead Sea. The waters of this stream will make the salty waters of the Dead Sea fresh and pure. There will be swarms of living things wherever the water of this river flows. Fish will abound in the Dead Sea, for its waters will become fresh. Life will flourish wherever this water flows. Fishermen will stand along the shores of the Dead Sea. (Ezk. 47:6–10a NLT)

Please note, although this river is defined in the same way in Ezekiel 47:12, I have chosen to quote from Revelation.

> Then the angel showed me the river of the water of life, bright as crystal, flowing from the throne of God and of the Lamb through the middle of the street of the city; also, on either side of the river, the tree of life with its twelve kinds of fruit, yielding its fruit each month. The leaves of the tree were for the healing of the nations. (Rev. 22:1–2)

> The leaves of these trees will never turn brown and fall, and there will always be fruit on their branches. (Ezk. 47:12b NLT)

Commentator William Hendriksen suggests, "The term 'tree of life' is collective, just like 'avenue' and 'river.' ... there is not just one single tree. No, there is an entire park: whole rows of trees alongside the river."[2]

Adam and Eve were banned from *this tree* after they sinned and *in a sense* this contributed to their deaths.

The life-preserving river and its trees reflect Jesus' very

nature. Just as we experienced Him on earth, healing, satisfying and relieving, Jesus always has and will provide for our every need and longing.

SURROUNDINGS

Down the mountain from the temple and River of Life there would undoubtedly be a beautiful plaza. This plaza would be used to provide (or coordinate) the staging of worshippers and sacrifices prior to their entry into the temple.

Such might require auxiliary areas adjacent to the plaza with pens for the animals and hotels or billets for distant visitors. As you might imagine, these areas might comprise a significant *township* with all the shops and accommodations.

Various OT believers (or priests) could assure the appropriateness of peoples' preparedness as well as the sacrificial animals. In one sense, the scene would be similar to temple scenes at Christ's first advent. However, none of the corruption that existed then would be permitted (or even thought of).

He will judge the world with justice, and the nations with his truth. (Psa. 96:13c)

TEMPLE WORSHIP

Jesus will establish the worship as described in Ezekiel. Believers will come to worship Christ directly and to bring Him gifts. Some form of memorial sacrifices will be offered, primarily lambs. This will undoubtedly surprise some (and it has been a debated issue) but this is what is

CHRIST'S KINGDOM

described in Ezekiel 43. This will not be expiatory but a memorial to Jesus' sacrifice. It is unclear how this worship scene will extend to the world of Gentile believers. Its primary focus is the Israelis – all of whom will believe!

Whether Jesus will permit other temples within the land of Israel is unclear. If so, they could participate in the ritual worship of their Lord. He could deploy representative priests and could appear in the other temples supernaturally to provide the personalized worship that all would desire.

Leaders from around the world will come to pay homage, worship and seek His teaching and infinitely wise counsel.

> "Come, let us go up to the mountain of the LORD, to the house of the God of Jacob, that he may teach us his ways and that we may walk in his paths." For out of Zion shall go the law, and the word of the LORD from Jerusalem. (Isa. 2:2, 3)

Homage, indeed, will be required of the nations.

> In the end, the enemies of Jerusalem who survive the plague *(during the Great Tribulation)* will go up to Jerusalem each year to worship the King, the Lord of Heaven's Armies, and to celebrate the Festival of Shelters (during the Millennium). Any nation in the world that refuses to come to Jerusalem to worship the King, the Lord of Heaven's Armies, will have no rain. If the people of Egypt refuse to attend the festival, the Lord will punish them with the same plague that he sends on the other nations who refuse to go. (Zec. 14:16–18)

Those appearing before Jesus would experience Him in all His glory as they bowed before our Lord. They would be prostrating themselves in fear, reverence and awe. These mortals would be in the presence of one who appeared as He did on the Mount of Transfiguration. Each in attendance would know they were completely exposed and vulnerable before the God and Creator of our universe.

KINGDOM WORSHIP

Jesus could instruct His Bride Saints as to how to set up churches or temples around the world as well as the worship services. This would be part of their priestly duties.

Certainly this would not be a one-time event. One or more Bride Saints could be assigned to each of the temples or churches as prescribed by the Lord. (cf. Rev. 5:10, 20:6)

The mysterious aspect of this is: What system of worship would Jesus desire? Would temple sacrifices extend beyond Israel? Which of the festivals would Israel celebrate and would the Gentile nations follow in kind (or perform some variation thereof). The Bible is mostly silent with this regard.

As His worship centers are set up, relics of all other religions must be destroyed: i.e., idols, shrines, mosques, synagogues and cathedrals must all be put to the torch. Concurrent with this, all non-biblical religious books and related written materials must be destroyed as well. This will be a momentous task requiring a concerted on-going activity until all remnants are gone.

In addition every cultic, devil worship and variants of witchcraft (buildings, literature, idols etc.) must be torched. The earth must be rid of every vestiges of false religious or satanic objects. *Bulldozers and flamethrowers come to mind!*

CHRIST'S KINGDOM

CHRIST'S REIGN

Jesus will reign from His temple (literally from on-high). He will have re-established Edenic conditions throughout earth, having lifted the curse from all. (Revelation 22:3). So, beginning with Israel, the earth will yield its fruits without the toil (over such things as weeds) which plagued mankind for millennia.

> Tell all the nations, "The Lord reigns!" The world stands firm and cannot be shaken. He will judge all peoples fairly. Let the heavens be glad, and the earth rejoice! Let the sea and everything in it shout his praise! Let the fields and their crops burst out with joy! Let the trees of the forest rustle with praise before the Lord, for he is coming! (Psa. 96:10–13a NLT)

> Even the wilderness and desert will be glad in those days. The wasteland will rejoice and blossom with spring crocuses. Yes, there will be an abundance of flowers and singing and joy! The deserts will become as green as the mountains of Lebanon, as lovely as Mount Carmel or the Plain of Sharon. There the Lord will display his glory, the splendor of our God (Isa. 35:1–2)

Governmentally, Jesus will establish His theocracy per His specifications. His resurrected saints will reign with Him providing perfect, non-corrupt leadership and law enforcement.

> For to us a child is born, to us a son is given, and the government will be on his shoulders. And he will be called Wonderful Counselor, Mighty God, Everlasting Father, Prince of Peace. Of the increase of his government and peace there will be no end. He will reign on David's throne and over his kingdom, establishing and upholding it with justice and righteousness from that time on and forever. The zeal of the LORD Almighty will accomplish this. (Isa. 9:6–7 NIV)

BEYOND THE RAPTURE

> In my vision at night I looked, and there before me was one like a son of man, coming with the clouds of heaven. He approached the Ancient of Days and was led into his presence. He was given authority, glory and sovereign power; all nations and peoples of every language worshiped him. His dominion is an everlasting dominion that will not pass away, and his kingdom is one that will never be destroyed. (Dan. 7:13-14 NIV)

Psalm 72:1–19 provides an overall description of the reign of Christ. There are a multitude of verses which describe the facets and qualities of Jesus' reign.

One can get a preliminary sense of how Jesus' reign will impact Israel (and in the larger sense the entire world), by reading how magnificent the reign of Solomon was.

> The people of Judah and Israel were as numerous as the sand on the seashore; they ate, they drank and they were happy. And Solomon ruled over all the kingdoms from the Euphrates River to the land of the Philistines, as far as the border of Egypt. These countries brought tribute and were Solomon's subjects all his life. (1 Kin. 4:20-21 NIV)

> He ruled over all the kingdoms west of the Euphrates River, from Tiphsah to Gaza, and had peace on all sides. During Solomon's lifetime Judah and Israel, from Dan to Beersheba, lived in safety, everyone under their own vine and under their own fig tree. (1 Kin. 4:24-25 NIV)

Following is a terse list of that which will typify Christ's Millennium:

- Peace (between nations, tribes, ethnicities, individuals)
- Beauty beyond measure
- Righteousness experienced by the majority
- Abundance
- Law and order

CHRIST'S KINGDOM

- Societal fairness
- Justice (thoroughly enforced)
- Healthiness
- True knowledge of God
- Universal worship of our Triune God
- Productivity – meaningful labor
- Freedom in a multitude of ways
- Joyfulness
- Prosperity

NOTE: This list was derived from *Things to Come* (Dwight Pentecost).

Jesus will function as Redeemer (Isa. 49:10–21, 62:11, Mal 4:2), Judge of all saints (Isa. 62:12), Monarch/teacher (Isa. 2:3, Zec. 8:22), our King (Isa. 2:3, Zec. 8:22), King 5:2–5, Zep. 3:15), Prophet (Deu. 18:15, 18), Giver of the law (Isa. 33:22, Gen. 49:10), and the Great Shepherd (Isa. 40:10–11; Jer. 23:1, 3, Mic. 4:5, 7:14)

One can get a further sense of how the whole world responds to Christ's reign (to a slight degree) by reading about Solomon's court:

> King Solomon was greater in riches and wisdom than all the other kings of the earth. The whole world sought audience with Solomon to hear the wisdom God had put in his heart. Year after year, everyone who came brought a gift — articles of silver and gold, robes, weapons and spices, and horses and mules. (1 Kin. 10:23-25)

CHRIST'S WORLD DESIGN

So now Christ would rearrange earth as He desires. Christ could soon place Survivor saints in strategic places around the earth (cf. Isa. 10:20, 21) and distribute animal life.

> For all creation is waiting eagerly for that future day when God will reveal who his children really are. Against its will, all creation was subjected to God's curse. But with eager hope, the creation looks forward to the day <u>when it will join God's children in glorious freedom</u> from death and decay. (Romans 8:19–21 NLT)

Beauty will be the hallmark of the earth. All will echo the goodness of God. Everything will exalt Him. Next, Christ may establish towns, cities, states and countries. Concurrent with that, He will set up government as He directs Survivor saints and creatures to their new locations.

Languages and laws will be established. All societal rules will be handed down for newly-established governing authorities to enforce. *Read Psalms 46 through 48 for descriptions of Christ's reign.* Following is a rich passage from Psalm 47:

> For God is the King over all the earth. Praise him with a psalm! God reigns above the nations, sitting on his holy throne. The rulers of the world have gathered together with the people of the God of Abraham. For all the kings of the earth belong to God. He is highly honored everywhere. (Psa. 47:7–9)

The new earth (free of the curse) will be spectacular! Flowers, trees, skies and seas will all have a beauty beyond compare. Many pebbles will be gems. Beautiful birds and butterflies will abound.

Churches will be built and universal Christianity established. As Christ's resurrected saints participate in all of this, they may be ministering to the believers who have entered the Millennium. Due to the extreme conditions evoked by the persecution of the Antichrist and God's fury, many will be in desperate straits ... sick, wounded and maimed. According to Isaiah, the Lord will heal them all, beginning with the Jews. It will be thrilling to experience

> When he comes, he will open the eyes of the blind and unplug the ears of the deaf. The lame will leap like a deer, and those who cannot speak will sing for joy! (Isa. 35:5-6 NLT)

EARLY ACTIVITIES OF THE RESURRECTED

At sometime during all these preceding activities, there would be wondrous reunions of Christian relatives and friends who had died or been raptured. Particularly wonderful will be parents getting reconnected with their infants and young children who died prematurely. The resurrected will discover generations of believers in their families (past and *future*).

There will be wonderful surprises – friends who became believers after they *parted company*. Even more wonderful will be those who became believers – those we were sure had *gone to hell*. Many reconciliations will take place (brethren, family, or spouses). Furthermore it is possible that mortals too, may be allowed to get acquainted with relatives who are now Bride Saints or OT saints.

We will become reacquainted with those we have influenced for Christ; for instance, *Spiritual children* we led to Christ or influenced to become believers.

> After all, what gives us hope and joy, and what will be our proud reward and crown as we stand before the Lord Jesus when He returns? It is you. (1The. 2:19 NLT)

Our 'friends in Heaven appear to be those whose lives

we have touched on Earth and who now have their own *eternal dwellings*. Luke 16:9 seems to say these 'eternal dwellings' of our friends are places where we'll stay and enjoy companionship – second homes to us as we move about the kingdom." [3]

We will have the joy of seeing others made whole (those previously crippled or deformed). Others who were mentally handicapped will be healed. Many will be freed of personality quirks and disorders. Every undesirable aspect and trait will be gone forever.

"For 3 things I thank God every day of my life; thanks; that he has vouchsafed me knowledge of his works; deep thanks that he has set in my darkness the lamp of faith; deep, deepest thanks that I have another life to look forward to, a life joyous with light and flowers and heavenly song."

Helen Keller (both blind and deaf from birth)

At least 70% of today's population is under oppressive dictatorial reigns. Think of China and Russia; have these people ever experienced freedom?

Many Christians have been suffering for their faith during our lifetime. Bride Saints coming from these brutal situations will be jubilant at being completely free (free from personal and religious oppression), There will probably be special celebrations of martyrs and Tribulation saints who suffered terribly and triumphed.

Numerous Bride Saints will never have experienced freedom in their entire lives on earth. Perhaps the OT and NT celebrities and heroes of the faith will be feted (see Hebrews 11, *the hall of faith*, and the book of Job wherein

CHRIST'S KINGDOM

God, Himself, extolled Job for his righteous life.)

In the year 1546 Philip Melanchthon spoke of his friend, Martin Luther, in a commemorative speech. Philip envisioned him in Heaven spending time with notables of the faith. "We remember the great delight with which he recounted the course, the counsels, perils and the escapes of the prophets and the learning which he discoursed on all the ages of the church thereby showing that he was inflamed by no ordinary passion for these wonderful men. Now he embraces them and rejoices to hear them speak and to speak to them in turn. Now they hail him gladly as a companion and thank God with him for having gathered and preserved the Church." [4]

How Jesus will orchestrate all this is difficult to imagine. Perhaps there will be ongoing celebrations with different groupings from various eras or situations.

On a sad note, we will discover that certain friends and relatives we expected to be present but are not! As a reference, you can read Jesus' parable about the wheat and the tares in Mat 13:29–30, 36–42. Also consider the following verse:

> Not everyone who says to me, "Lord, Lord," will enter the kingdom of Heaven, but the one who does the will of my Father who is in Heaven ..." (Mat. 7:21a)

You may wish to read the remainder of this passage in Matthew 7:21–23.

I realize that there is the perception there will be no more tears or sadness, but upon considering all that will be happening in the Millennium (for example: the millions rallying to Satan's war cry at the end), I believe that we will continue to experience these emotions throughout the era but with the ever-present comfort of our Savior. The time of constant joy (and no sadness) will occur with the New Heaven and Earth.

---

1. Merrill F. Unger, "The Temple Visions of Ezekiel," *Bibliotheca Sacra*, 106:48–57

2 William Hendriksen, *More Than Conquerors*, 249

3 Randy Alcorn, *Heaven*, 248

4 Philip Melanchthon

CHAPTER 5

BRIDE SAINTS

The Bride of Christ or bride, the Lamb's wife is a term used in reference to a group of related verses in the Bible—in the Gospels, Revelation, the Epistles and related verses in the Old Testament. Sometimes the Bride is implied through calling Jesus a Bridegroom. For over fifteen hundred years the Church was identified as the bride betrothed to Christ.[1]

The subject of the Bride of Christ has been one of intrigue down through the 2000-year Church Age. For a tremendously large group of believers to be given this singular title and for we as individual Christians to imagine what that means for us causes untold puzzlement. Therefore I have tried to not be among the faint-hearted and have endeavored to render a biblically reasonable explanation.

In this chapter, I will touch on various aspects of our lives as immortal Bride-Saints: our emotional experience, our immortal bodies, our personalities, our mortal marriages, our capabilities, our fellowship, our relationship to angels, our ministries and our interactions with mortals. *By the way, this portion of the book was the first topic I tackled and led to its creation.*

IMMEASURABLE JOY

Astonishment, gratefulness, joy and awe will reverberate endlessly through the NT Bride Saints. Far surpassing the thrill of holding a new-born or the embrace of newly-weds, it will bond us together and yet, lift each in ongoing elation.

> God raised us up with him and seated us with him in the heavenly places in Christ Jesus, so that in the coming ages he might show the immeasurable riches of his grace in kindness toward us in Christ Jesus. (Eph. 2:6-7)

As I mentioned previously, our new bodies will be immortal bodies. *Before reading what I have written about our lives as Bride Saints, you might want to reference Appendix D, Spiritual Beings.*

> He will take our weak mortal bodies and change them into glorious bodies like his own, using the same power with which he will bring everything under his control. (Php. 3:21 NLT)

Jesus will grant us total access to Himself. We may have some form of physical contact as well (ala the Apostle John who rested against Jesus' chest).

We will be completely in touch with the Holy Spirit and God the Father like Jesus was (as described in the Gospels). We will be so fully in tune with them that it will totally eclipse anything we knew or even imagined during our lives on earth. This will enable us to manifest an overarching, agape love to each and every mortal we encounter.

> What joy for those you choose to bring near, those who live in your holy courts. What festivities await us inside your holy Temple. (Psa. 65:4 NLT)

We will have intimate face to face visits with Jesus (individually and collectively). On an even more intimate level, Jesus might sing to His bride. Our God's music could

BRIDE SAINTS

be with angelic accompaniment and an orchestra which would be incredible. (cf. Mat. 26:30)

> For the Lord your God is living among you. He is a mighty savior. He will take delight in you with gladness. With his love, he will calm all your fears. He will rejoice over you with joyful songs. (Zep. 3:17 NLT).

NOTE: In context, this verse pertains to God's joy over redeemed Israel.

We will each have a new name given to us by Jesus.

> To the one who conquers I will give some of the hidden manna, and I will give him a white stone, with a new name written on the stone that no one knows except the one who receives it. (Rev. 2:17c)

I take this to be a wonderful pet name which Jesus will call us when we interact with him personally. God renamed several individuals in the Bible (Abraham, Sarah, Jacob and Peter). He did so in what could be called a prophetic manner. Our new name mentioned here seems significantly different.

NEW IMMORTAL BODIES

The Bride Saints will have Christ-like bodies. However, although we are God-like, we will not possess those three incredible attributes of God: omnipotence, omnipresence and omniscience (plus a number of His other qualities). But we will have glorious new capabilities.

> Beloved, we are God's children now, and what we will be has not yet appeared; but we know that when he appears we shall be like him, because we shall see him as he is. (1John 3:2)

BEYOND THE RAPTURE

In a prayer by David, he says, "I praise you, for I am fearfully and wonderfully made. Wonderful are your works." (Psa. 139:14) We will be forever grateful for our incredible resurrection bodies.

Taking a hint from what Paul says about the difference between a seed and that which sprouts and develops (in 1 Corinthians 15:35–44), we can begin to grasp the magnitude of differences between our mortal and immortal bodies. Recall the small, unattractive and nondescript appearance of a seed, and then think of the resultant, beautiful flowers which bloom on any number of plants of varying structure and size.

Take for example roses: From a seed there develops a thorny structure. Yet such bear spectacular flowers of a multiplicity of colors and blends of hues (and God has added to that a variety of marvelous fragrances).

Paul gives us several other intriguing examples, yet provides no further information. So God must chuckle time after time as we struggle to perceive what a glorious immortal body might be like.

Then there is the matter of the various crowns awarded different saints. Are different crowns worn on different occasions or does God combine the crowns in some wonderful manner? Another alternative might be that they manifest as beautiful colorful halos. Granted, we throw our crowns at Christ's feet but I suspect He returns them to us to wear as He intended.

You and I could go on and on listing the beautiful attributes that God might endow upon us, yet we remain somewhat teased and mildly perplexed as we try to imagine how God will render the various aspects of our immortal bodies. As I conclude writing about this puzzle (and you puzzle through what I have written), I do hope we amused each member of our beloved Triune Godhead or invoked a smile.

OUR NEW SPIRITUAL PERSONALITIES

In our immortal bodies, we will not sin AND there is no double jeopardy! We can never sin again! How marvelous it will be to be freed from our sin nature. Our joy will be immeasurable as we are freed to love and serve God (and each other) as we were meant to. It will be a thrill to become that perfect a person – what we always wanted to be and much, much more.

> But our High Priest offered himself to God as a single sacrifice for sins, good for all time. Then he sat down in the place of honor at God's right hand. For by that one offering he <u>forever made perfect those who are being made holy.</u> (Heb. 10:14, 16)

We will be joyous, wise and loving (Christ-like). We will be humble despite our glorious new identities.

> But the fruit of the Spirit is love, joy, peace, patience, kindness, goodness, faithfulness, gentleness, self-control; against such things there is no law. (Gal. 5:22–23)

I believe each person will be recognizable, with features like we had in our early thirties (or younger). Of course that would not be the case with children, who might appear as they were. The exception would be miscarried babies (or the like). I think they would probably appear as two to five year old children. Whether immortal beings of this stature would then grow to adulthood, remains to be seen.

BEYOND THE RAPTURE

These ideas come from two *near-death experience* books, *90 Minutes in Heaven* by Dan Piper and *Heaven is For Real* by Todd Burpo.

Each of our personas must certainly be preserved. Those characteristics that define you will remain, though greatly refined (personality, preferences, interests, giftedness et al). When Christ reestablishes each one of us in immortal form, all of our endearing, interesting and desirable qualities will be embodied in a magnificent, resplendent being – a being who pleases God, ourselves and all other heavenly beings.

I think *Bride* women will retain their femininity and *Bride* men their manhood, yet without specific sexual features.

We may be clothed in light. This may be what the Gospel writers were trying to describe when Jesus was transfigured. I have long wondered if Adam and Eve were clothed with light before they sinned and discovered themselves to be naked.

We will have eternal bodies (food, drink and sleep could be optional). It is shown in Scripture that even angels and God Himself (when they manifested themselves as humans) partook of human meals (cf. Gen. 18:1–2, 5–8). In Psalms, manna is called the *bread of angels*. (cf. Psa. 78:25).

I do not find it specifically mentioned that we eat of the Tree of Life, but we certainly may.

MARRIAGE SURPASSED

Three things will last forever – faith, hope, and love – and

BRIDE SAINTS

the greatest of these is love. (1 Cor. 13:13)

In the Millennium, we are the Bride of Christ. We will have new spiritual bodies (cf. 1 Cor. 15:35-50) with no logical need to procreate; but we will be deeply involved in the spiritual births of people throughout the Millennium.

For in the resurrection they neither marry nor are given in marriage, but are like angels in Heaven. (Mat. 22:30)

INTIMACY

Sex will no longer be needed, desirable or, for that matter, possible.

The above concepts might shock some of you who are still trying to transition mentally from being mortal to being immortal. I know that my wife and I have wrestled with the question of what becomes of our marriage in Heaven.

Unfortunately, the Bible is silent with this regard (other than the statement referenced above). Some couples achieve intimacy that transcends physical romance and companionship. We feel we have achieved that but what will become of our relationship in the Millennium and then in the New Earth?

I suspect that married couples will be given a very special eternal bond that will soar far beyond all the joys of marriage on earth. They will be eternally intertwined in this relationship. One might imitate those who asked Jesus a similar question (just prior to Christ's answer in Matthew 22:30) and ask about widowed Christians who married other Christians? I would recommend we leave that to God. I believe He will resolve this in a marvelously satisfactory fashion.

BEYOND THE RAPTURE

OUR CAPABILITES

We will have total connectivity and great fellowship with other Bride Saints (supernaturally). Being incomparably superior to our persona today, we will each be perfect, loving and lovable.

I would like to believe that each of us will have all the giftedness and capabilities we had hoped for on earth. For example, those who had wanted to be a talented artist, athlete, musician, etcetera, would now have those capabilities (to perfection).

Our magnificent eternal immortal bodies will be equally adapted to both worlds – mortal and spiritual. Our bodies will never age or die. They will be similar but vastly superior to mortal flesh – without a sin nature. We will not be inhibited by walls, gravity, storms or water. Even intentional invisibility might serve us. Our minds will outperform the most brilliant minds today or any of today's computers. We will be impervious to attacks of any kind (ala Luke 10:19). But do realize our very existence will continue to be sustained by our Lord and Savior (cf. Heb. 1:3).

New senses will be added to our five human senses to accommodate our new capabilities and the new dimensionality of our spiritual bodies. I say this with the Scriptures (cf. 1Cor. 15:35–55) in mind and more specifically this portion:

> So is it with the resurrection of the dead. What is sown is perishable; <u>what is raised is imperishable</u>. It is sown in dishonor; <u>it is raised in glory</u>. It is sown in weakness; <u>it is raised in power</u>. It is sown a natural body; <u>it is raised a spiritual body</u>. If there is a natural body, there is also a

BRIDE SAINTS

spiritual body. (1 Cor. 15:42–44)

With our new capabilities, it is reasonable to expect we will be learning and using different languages. There are a great many languages around the earth these days. Bible translators have yet to translate the Bible into a great number of them. I doubt we'll be learning bunches of these. But for the Bride Saints, I imagine the important ones will be the language of Heaven and the angels (cf. 1 Cor. 13:1) plus Hebrew. Adding these languages to our capabilities will probably not be a taxing effort but should be an easy matter with our new God-provided eternal bodies.

Our means of transportation would be supernatural – perhaps that white horse we rode to earth with Jesus to ride above and upon earth.

> Then I saw Heaven opened, and a white horse was standing there. Its rider was named Faithful and True, for he judges fairly and wages a righteous war. ... The armies of Heaven, dressed in the finest of pure white linen, <u>followed him on white horses</u>. (Rev. 19:11–14)

Reading this verse you realize that these words are describing a supernatural event. Christ's army and their steeds are spiritual creatures. They are able to descend from Heaven to earth in a supernatural manner.

Another venue of transportation might be dolphins or Orcas in the sea. My wife and I have been entertained and then *ferried* by dolphins in the large porpoise pools used to entertain tourists in Cabo San Lucas, Mexico.

<u>OUR FELLOWSHIP</u>

We will necessarily have our own exclusive worship

system. Because of our direct (individual and collective) relationship with Jesus, there will be beautiful ceremonies of face to face worship of our Triune God. To include mortals, OT saints or even angels may not be appropriate! We will do so in ethereal manner, singing to *them* and they to us. The meaningfulness of communion will transcend anything imagined. The exact nature of the overall rituals of worship will remain a mystery until we are there.

The potential scope of our fellowship in the Millennium is utterly mind-boggling. As if direct fellowship with our Triune Godhead were not sufficient in itself, we will have fellowship (pure and complete) with our Bride-saint relatives (many of whom lived before we were born), Bride-saint friends, other Bride Saints, OT saints, NT and OT notables and angels.

One of the exciting prospects will be to be able to dialog with the Apostles and other direct disciples of Jesus. The following verse comes to mind with that regard:

> Jesus also did many other things. If they were all written down, I suppose the whole world could not contain the books that would be written. (John 21:25 NLT)

I, for one, am quite desirous to hear (and dote upon) many firsthand accounts about Jesus' ministry. I would also love to hear of how the *explosion* of Christianity occurred at the hands of the Apostles.

Aside: one interesting question to be answered is who will be the twelfth apostle to rule the tribes of Israel – Paul or Matthias? The following idea might be the answer. Matthias could be the twelfth apostle to the Israelis whereas Paul could continue to be the apostle to the Gentiles. He could be the organizational head and spiritual guide to the entire world of Gentile believers. In a sense he deserves this, considering his astounding ministry, sacrifice and contributions to the Bible.

ANGELS

We will be able to see and interact with angels (they might serve us) but mortals probably will not be able to see them. Perhaps Christ will make an exception when He grants special audiences to mortals.

Although angels are a mystery to us today due to their invisible qualities and are incredibly powerful and able to see and serve God directly, they are: "... only servants – spirits sent to care for people who will inherit salvation." (Heb. 1:14 NLT)

You have made them *(us mortals)* a little lower than the angels and crowned them with glory and honor. (Psa. 8:5 NIV)

As mentioned previously, we will be given the privilege of judging Satan's evil angels and perhaps allowed to give input as to their eternal sentences (there will be varying degrees of torture in Hell).

Do you not know that we are to judge angels? (1 Cor. 6:3)

We may get to *see* God's angels serving mortals (without their knowing it). Angels' roles would differ because they would no longer be battling demons. God might grant us the privilege of showing us how His angels battled for us (against evil angels) during ours and others' lifetimes.

We know that God designated angels to serve us during our stay on earth. So it will be a wonderful privilege to meet those who have protected us, accompanied us and acted on our behalf from childhood on. Hopefully they will remember the delightful things about us and forget all our shortcomings and stupid actions.

OUR MINISTRIES

We will be mysterious and God-like to mortals (cf. 1 John 3:2). Yet we will serve as glorious examples for Millennial mortals to observe. Hopefully this will cause them to aspire to become not *just* Christians but sacrificially strong Christians.

Being totally in touch with God, we may receive knowledge about each person (individually) and who they are by name and history (like Jesus with the woman at the well).

We will know how to relate to them and meet their needs. With these qualities we will serve God and mortals (non-Christians especially) in important ways.

Even when we are *established* in the Millennium, it may take us a while to "know what is the hope to which he has called you, what are the riches of his glorious inheritance in the saints," (Eph. 1:18c)

INTERACTIONS WITH MORTALS

Because we are part of the Bride of Christ, we are royalty, God's royalty! Therefore, each and every appearance we make in our roles as priests and rulers will be in the manner of royalty today; we will not fraternize with the people we serve, ala many professionals whom we experience today – doctors, judges and police

BRIDE SAINTS

The previous statement is speculative. John Walvoord states, "It may be demonstrated from Scripture ... objections to commingling of resurrected with non-resurrected are unjustified." [2]

So it is entirely possible for there to be more informal interaction between resurrected beings and mortals. Dr. Walvoord does state that "As far as Scriptural revelation is concerned it *(resurrected saints' activities)* seems limited to a few specific functions, and the primary activity of the resurrected saints will be in the new and heavenly city." [3]

"Though the free mingling of resurrected and non-resurrected beings is contrary to our present experience there is no valid reason why there should not be a limited amount of such association in the millennial earth." [4]

However we interface with mankind, the love of Christ will exude from us. Every pronouncement we utter will impact our subjects with the type of awe people had for the wisdom and love Christ shared with the Israelites.

Thus we will represent Christ to them perfectly and of course this does not preclude their being in His presence at various times.

INTERACTIONS AS RULERS

Christ will rule with a *rod of iron* (cf. Rev. 19:15) through his Bride Saints and angels (to a certain degree – in other critical matters, He will take action directly)! For all involved, this will be a no-nonsense approach yet infused and enforced with agape love. Just as in the life of nations today, true freedom, justice and peace must be defended aggressively. The sin nature of mankind will continue to demand such *police* action in the Millennium. So Jesus will not permit grand-scale sin or in any quarter. Instead, He will set up (and enforce) a perfect governmental system.

There will be no war. More importantly, the *peace of Christ* will now transcend from inner peace to worldwide peace. Something few of us have ever known!

As rulers at every level of government under Christ (with the exception of Israel), we will probably have representative mortals (who are believers) who carry out our orders (for our jurisdiction). They could in turn come to us for feedback and correction, as we observe the results of their efforts. *Please see the section on Government in Chapter 9 for further details.*

INTERACTIONS AS JUDGES

As Bride Saints, we will be able to judge court cases easily and correctly due to our ability to discern the thoughts and intents of all involved.

INTERACTIONS AS PRIESTS

We may structure and oversee mortals' worship of our Lord. We might be able to give testimony of how God saved us and cared for us during our lives as humans.

We may be able to perform miracles to accomplish God's purposes.

We will be great counselors, albeit through the leadership of the church. Of course we will be directing such leaders on how best to extend the love and mercy of Christ,

BRIDE SAINTS

And many peoples shall come, and say: "Come, let us go up to the mountain of the LORD, to the house of the God of Jacob, that he may teach us his ways and that we may walk in his paths." (Isa. 2:3)

BRIDE SAINTS OVERALL MINISTRY

I for one, was looking to the Millennium as a heavenly respite from the trials of earthly living, but now see it as a time for the ingathering of innumerable saints for God's pleasure and kingdom. It will not (should not) be a time to *kick back* and lounge.

Rather it will be a time of intense effort for the kingdom of God. Granted we will have new bodies with marvelous capabilities, but I think this will be one fulfillment of throwing our crowns at Christ's feet. That is, we will set aside luxuriating in the *lap of God* to serve Him in ways far superior to when we were earth-bound.

We will rule as He wants and sacrificially give ourselves to the advancement of soul winning and discipleship. This would be consistent with the work that our Triune God and their angels will be doing throughout this era.

We will be much more preoccupied with serving God and mortals than ourselves.

But do not think that this will be one thousand years of *nothing* but exhaustive work. God rested on the seventh day (Genesis 2:2). This (and the laws that God decreed) established for all time the concept of a Sabbath rest (for both man and beast). Therein He invoked the observation of days, weeks and even years of rest (Lev. 25:4–5). Therefore we should expect times of rest in the

BEYOND THE RAPTURE

Millennium.

Of course, we will have had a significant time of uninterrupted, wondrous communion with Jesus during The Tribulation.

---

1 Wikipedia, *Bride of Christ*.

2 Walvoord, 324

3 *ibid*. 329

4 *ibid*. 330

CHAPTER 6

ISRAEL

We have all shaken our heads at the resolute stance most Jews take against belief in their Messiah. It is quite heartbreaking to experience their stubbornness. But now let us examine the marvelous way God plans to shower them with His unmerited love and esteem in The Millennium.

> Behold, the days are coming, declares the LORD, when I will raise up for David a righteous Branch, and he shall reign as king and deal wisely, and shall execute justice and righteousness in the land. In his days Judah will be saved, and Israel will dwell securely. And this is the name by which he will be called: "The LORD is our righteousness." (Jer. 23:5)

Scripturally speaking, this chapter should precede the one about Bride Saints. However, being a Gentile, I favored placing us first. But of greater importance are the Jews and the land of Israel. There is a considerable amount written about the Jews and Israel (and little about Gentile believers) regarding the Millennium.

Discovering God's unmerited yet abiding love and favor for the Jews left me marveling and stunned in a sense. But it should not leave any of us surprised. After all, God chose Israel to be the one nation through whom He would embrace all of humanity. He effectively used them to establish His message to the world and to provide the Savior. For that reason, Satan has done everything in his power to assail and destroy the Jew and to make the Jew the object of hatred and condemnation worldwide. One scholar of centuries past has stated their history past, present and future quite eloquently:

"The Jews may be considered in three states infinitely different: the first, is that which they were in before Messiah; the second, is that which they have held, and still hold, since the death of Messiah, in consequence of having rejected him, and much more, of having obstinately persisted in their unbelief; the <u>third</u> is yet future, nor is it known when it shall be. In these three states are they frequently regarded and spoken of in scripture;

"<u>In the first state, before Messiah</u>, the scriptures regard them: First, as the owners and legitimate masters of all that portion of the earth which God himself gave to their fathers in solemn and perpetual gift: "All the land which thou seest, to thee will I give it, and to thy seed forever," Gen 15:18 and 13:15. Secondly, it considers them as the only people of God, or which is the same as his church. Thirdly, as a true and lawful spouse of God himself, whose espousals were solemnly celebrated in the wilderness of Mount Sinai, Exodus 19 and Ezekiel 23. Fourthly, it considers them as endued with another kind of life infinitely more valuable than natural life.

"<u>In the second state, after Messiah</u>, it considers them: First, as disinherited of their native land, scattered to every wind, and abandoned to the contempt and derision, and hatred, and barbarity of all nations. Secondly, as deprived of the honour and dignity of the people of God, as if God himself were no longer their God. Thirdly, as a faithless and most ungrateful spouse, ignominiously cast forth from the house of her husband, despoiled of all her attire and precious jewels, which had been heaped upon her with such profusion, and enduring the greatest hardships and miseries in her solitude, in her dishonour, in her total abandonment of Heaven and earth. Fourthly, it regards them as deprived of that life which so highly distinguished them from all the living

"In the third state still future, but infallibly believed and expected, Divine Scripture regards them: First, as gathered again, by the omnipotent arm of the living God, from among all the peoples and nations of the world, as restored to their own land, and reestablished in it, not to be removed forever." "Secondly, it regards them as restored with the highest honour, and with the greatest advantages," "Thirdly, it considers them as a spouse of God . . .

"These three estates of the Jews perfectly correspond to the three states of the life of holy Job, which we may regard as a figure, or as a history written in cypher of the three mighty revolutions of the people of God."[1]

Now I presume to continue where the previous quotes left off, by describing with Scripture the incredible inheritance God will be giving to Israel and the Jews:

> I will take you from the nations and gather you from all the countries and bring you into your own land. I will sprinkle clean water on you, and you shall be clean from all your uncleannesses, and from all your idols I will cleanse you. (Ezk 36:24–25)

We see that Christ purposes (prophetically) to ingather the remnant of Jews and to offer them salvation.

> And I will give you a new heart, and a new spirit I will put within you. And I will remove the heart of stone from your flesh and give you a heart of flesh. And I will put my Spirit within you, and cause you to walk in my statutes and be careful to obey my rules. (Ezk. 36:26–27)

BEYOND THE RAPTURE

The preceding verses describe that same conversion each believer experiences; but in this case, it is the entire Jewish remnant, in concert.

> Therefore, behold, I will allure her, and bring her into the wilderness, and speak tenderly to her. And there I will give her vineyards and make the Valley of Achor a door of hope. (Hos. 2:14–15a)
> She will give herself to me there, as she did long ago when she was young, when I freed her from her captivity in Egypt. When that day comes," says the Lord, "you will call me 'my husband' instead of 'my master.". (Hos. 2:15b–16 NLT)

The preceding verses describe the mystery of Israel becoming a wife to God. The following verses describe God's mercy on the Jews and their land, Israel.

> You shall dwell in the land that I gave to your fathers, and you shall be my people, and I will be your God. And I will deliver you from all your uncleannesses. And I will summon the grain and make it abundant and lay no famine upon you. I will make the fruit of the tree and the increase of the field abundant, that you may never again suffer the disgrace of famine among the nations. (Ezk. 36:28–30)

> In that day the branch of the LORD shall be beautiful and glorious, and the fruit of the land shall be the pride and honor of the survivors of Israel. And he who is left in Zion and remains in Jerusalem will be called holy, everyone who has been recorded for life in Jerusalem, when the Lord shall have washed away the filth of the daughters of Zion and cleansed the bloodstains of Jerusalem from its midst by a spirit of judgment and by a spirit of burning. (Isa. 4:2–4)

This Scripture describes how God resides in Israel and for Israel:

> Then the LORD will create over the whole site of Mount Zion and over her assemblies a cloud by day, and smoke and the shining of a flaming fire by night; for over all the

ISRAEL

glory there will be a canopy There will be a booth for shade by day from the heat, and for a refuge and a shelter from the storm and rain. (Isa. 4:5–6)

There is a large body of Scripture echoing descriptions such as these. Israel will become the "apple of God's eye." (cf. Zec. 3:17). He will make her resplendent! Everything of God and for God will flow through Israel with Jerusalem its Temple and capital.

Who is a God like you, pardoning iniquity and passing over transgression for the remnant of his inheritance? He does not retain his anger forever, because he delights in steadfast love.

He will again have compassion on us; he will tread our iniquities underfoot. You will cast all our sins into the depths of the sea. You will show faithfulness to Jacob and steadfast love to Abraham, as you have sworn to our fathers from the days of old. (Mic. 7:18–20)

"The Israelites who ... survive the great Tribulation ... will inherit the Promised Land and fulfill the hundreds of prophecies that have to do with Israel's hope in the Millennial kingdom. These promises are delineated in the Abrahamic, Davidic, Palestinian, and New Covenants." [2]

"In only a few instances these promises specifically are related to the New Heaven and the New Earth and constitute a description of the eternal state which follows the Millennium. (cf. Isa. 65:17, 18, 66:28) [3]

Israel is the primary nation to whom God has made such promises. However, Egypt and ancient Assyria (current day Iraq) will also be blessed in special ways.

In that day Egypt and Assyria will be connected by a highway. The Egyptians and Assyrians will move freely between their lands, and they will both worship God. And Israel will be their ally. The three will be together, and Israel will be a blessing to them. For the Lord of Heaven's Armies will say, "Blessed be Egypt, my people. Blessed be Assyria, the land I have made. Blessed be Israel, my special possession!" (Isa. 19:23–25 NLT)

I think Israel will be *action-central* in terms of Christianity (in general) and evangelism (in particular) during the Millennium. Whereas, Israel failed miserably in terms of turning Gentiles to God in the times preceding Christ's appearance; God will now use them to turn great multitudes of people to Himself (cf. Zec. 8:23).

One can get the sense of this by how God uses the 144,000 Jews to evangelize during the Tribulation. These Millennial Israelis will be primarily mortals. But God in His mercy and wisdom will probably use OT prophets and saints (immortals) to lead and guide their efforts.

NOTE: This is the impression one gets from commentaries on the passage about 144,000 Jews sealed for protection by God in Revelation 7:1–8 (which is followed by a resultant harvest of Tribulation martyrs [described in verses 9 and 10]).

The OT saints may minister to Israel in a manner similar to what Bride Saints will do for rest of the world.

REPLACEMENT "THEOLOGY"

There are a significant number of believers who spiritualize the idea of God having any future plans for Israel. Instead they believe that the church has replaced Israel.

I simply cannot understand how they can ignore so much definitive Scripture to the contrary. Their belief is

ISRAEL

called Replacement Theology. I hope this book will convince any who have been lead to believe this way to reconsider.

"The Church, the believing body of Jews and Gentiles, never nullified God's relationship with Israel. The rejection of Messiah put Israel's position on hold until a righteous generation was ready to accept the Messiah earlier rejected by most of Israel." [4]

If you are of the *Replacement persuasion,* I would encourage you to consider the following.

- Romans Chapters 9–11 detail God's eternal commitment to Israel and the Jewish.
- The fact that God's prophecies are always fulfilled.
- Ezekiel 40–48 and many other Millennial prophecies (a number of these are found in this document).
- The unconditional nature of the Abrahamic Covenant.

WORSHIP IN ISRAEL

Perhaps the OT prophets who labored so obediently will now be given the reward of working with a receptive and obedient Israel. They will be revered and loved (as they should have been when they labored so long ago). Of course each one of them will humbly deflect the adulation and refocus their subjects on their Lord and God. Israelites will be identified by tribes once again and the sons of Zadok (of the tribe of Levites) will act as priests. (cf. Ezk. 43:19, 40:46, 44:15–31, 45:15–16)

The worship system established in Israel will be significantly different from that which existed during

Christ's first advent. Ezekiel gives much information with this regard.

"There is no Ark of the Covenant, no Pot of Manna, no Aaron's rod to bud, no Tables of the Law, no Cherubim, no Mercy Seat, no golden Candlestick, no Shewbread, no Veil, no unapproachable Holy of Holies where the High-Priest might enter, nor is there any High-Priest..."[5]

There will be similarities between the Aaronic and millennial systems. In the Millennium, the worship centers about an altar (Ezk. 43:13–17) on which blood is sprinkled (43:18) and where the following sacrifices are offered: burnt offerings, sin offerings, and trespass offerings (40:39).

A person could spend much time in the Bible and read various authors to discover more intricate details about Temple Worship in the Millennium. I have only provided a few glimpses into what may be. *To view this in greater detail, review Ezekiel chapters 40–46.*

One of the intriguing mysteries of the Millennium is The Prince who will lead all of Israel's worship. Some have conjectured (and offered what they consider scriptural proof) that this is the resurrected David. It has been established that it is not Jesus through various things said about him. This great high priest will lead worship in Christ's temple and probably direct worship in the rest of Israel. Here is Scripture which speaks of him:

> All the people of Israel must join in bringing these offerings to the prince. The prince will be required to provide offerings that are given at the religious festivals. (Ezk. 45:16–17a NLT)

To read about this in detail, read Ezekiel chapters 45

ISRAEL

and 46.

ISRAEL'S GRATITUDE

Zechariah 12 (and in particular vs. 10) will be burned into Jews' minds.

And I will pour out on the house of David and the inhabitants of Jerusalem a spirit of grace and pleas for mercy, so that, when they look on me, on him whom they have pierced, they shall mourn for him, as one mourns for an only child, and weep bitterly over him, as one weeps over a firstborn. (Zec. 12:10)

None will ever forget the *mass realization* that *they* killed their Messiah and rejected Him at both a personal and national level. Coupled with that, they will remember with everlasting gratitude and reverence, how God kept His promise and rescued them for all eternity from Antichrist and all the nations bent on their destruction

One result will be that the Bride Saints will be doubly revered – first as Jesus' Bride and secondly as those who worshipped Him on earth and endeavored to win Jews to Jesus during the Church Age.

GOD'S COVENANTS

God's covenants are eternal (with the exception of the Mosaic covenant which is temporal). In the Millennium God fulfills the following covenants to Israel:

- The Abrahamic Covenant "made by God with Abraham is basic to the whole prophetic question. It is stated and confirmed unconditionally by God. (Gen. 12:103, 12:6–7, 13:14–17; 15:1–21, 17: 1–14; 22:15–18) ...promises made by Him to give to Abraham a land, a seed, and a blessing, which would be universal and eternal." [6]

.● The Davidic Covenant "is likewise unconditionally affirmed by God, promises a king, a kingdom, and a throne to the seed of Abraham AND promises an everlasting earthly kingdom over which David's son should reign. (cf. 2Sam. 7:12, Psa.89:3–4, Jer. 333:22, 25–26)." [7]

● The Palestinic Covenant "established by God gives the basis on which Israel will occupy and which was first given Abraham in the Abrahamic covenant," [8]

.● The New Covenant – provides a new heart, forgiveness of sin and filling of Holy Spirit. Jesus applies His New Covenant (as realized by Christians as a result of His First Advent) to the Jewish remnant en masse at the end of the Tribulation.

ISRAEL'S PEOPLE

The Jewish people will be prevalent in Israel. They will be the most accomplished and most revered of all mankind. Their country will be the model for all others. The official world language (or at least the language of worship and diplomacy) will be Hebrew.

> Then I will purify the speech of all people, so that everyone can worship the Lord together. (Zep. 3:9)

> In that day this song will be sung in the land of Judah: "We have a strong city; He sets up salvation as walls and bulwarks." (Isa. 26:1)

In that song, they exult in what God has done for them.

> "I will plant them on their land, and they shall never again be uprooted out of the land that I have given them," says

ISRAEL

the LORD your God. (Amos. 9:15)

Whole nations will desire to ally themselves to Israel in unabashed envy of their exalted position with God.

And many nations shall join themselves to the LORD in that day, and shall be my people. And I will dwell in your midst, and you shall know that the LORD of hosts has sent me to you. (Zec. 2:11)

Israel today benefits greatly from tourists interested in the history, ministry and travels of Jesus. Will the wonderful sites, cities, lakes and roads still be afforded worshippers and tourists in the Millennium? These days its visitors thrill to walk in Jesus' footsteps. The grandeur that will be Israel (during Christ's reign) will attract unimaginable numbers of people. All the superfluous buildings and memorials will have been removed. I would imagine the Lord will have restored each historic area to its original condition.

When Jesus reigns there, it will be a glorious privilege to retrace His footsteps knowing that each path and place was accurate and worthy of believers' adoring focus. I should think that everything in Jerusalem and surrounding will reverberate with His Righteousness and remind each person of their gracious God and Emperor. All will be astonished to see the degree to which Jesus has graced Israel.

To gain even more insight into how wonderfully God will restore Israel, read Isaiah chapter 60:16–22 and all of chapter 62.

JEWISH DEMOGRAPHICS

One of the incredible things about God's commitment

BEYOND THE RAPTURE

and promises to the Jews is the very small part of mankind they represent.

- There were 13.42 million Jews in the world in 2010, with 5.7 million in Israel, 5.3 million Jews in USA and about one million in Europe.

NOTE: these are 2010 statistics.

- Percentage-wise they are a minuscule part of the world. There are 7 billion people in the world now. At least 20% are Muslim, 1.4 billion strong; whereas Jews are only 16 hundredths of one percent (about 1000 Muslims for every Jew)!

- During WWII, there were concerted efforts to annihilate all Jews. Had not USA been provoked to enter the war, the outcome might have been disastrous (not only for the Jewish but for all freedom-loving peoples).

- At least 2,850,000 Jews were killed in the Soviet Union's by Stalin who killed between 20 and 45 million people overall.

- Hitler had 7,300,000 Jews killed in the holocaust (throughout Europe).

- The resultant death toll (above) was approximately ten million.

One could easily project that there would be three times the number of Jews today if Satan had not inflamed (or indwelt) madmen to commit genocide. He did so to thwart God's *plan of the ages* by trying to eradicate all Jews!

NOTABLE OT SAINTS

Many of the heroes of the faith and outstanding

ISRAEL

individuals in Biblical history will undoubtedly be given honor and special position in the Millennial Kingdom. I will mention those who come to mind: The Apostles, writers of the Bible, Mary and Joseph, John the Baptist, Abraham and Sarah, Isaac, Jacob, some of the godly kings of Israel, Moses, Joshua, King David, Samuel the prophet, Joseph, Gideon, Noah, Esther, Ruth and other of God's champions.

God has provided us His own list of OT notables in Hebrews chapter 11, which some term the *Hall of Faith*. You would gain from reading this entire chapter telling of these notables' faith and their anticipation of the Millennial Kingdom. I will quote from the last of it here:

> And what more shall I say? For time would fail me to tell of Gideon, Barak, Samson, Jephthah, of David and Samuel and the prophets – who through faith conquered kingdoms, enforced justice, obtained promises, . . . (Heb 11:32–33)

> They went about in skins of sheep and goats, destitute, afflicted, mistreated of whom the world was not worthy . . . (Heb. 11:37c–38a)

> All these people were still living by faith when they died. They did not receive the things promised; they only saw them and welcomed them from a distance, admitting that they were foreigners and strangers on earth. (Heb. 11:13 NIV)

To Daniel the prophet, God said:

> Go your way until the end. You will rest, and then at the end of the days, you will rise again to receive the inheritance set aside for you. (Dan. 12:13)

Roman Catholics may have had a correct perception of Mary as the Queen of Heaven, not in the way they deified her but that she will have a place of special honor for her role as the mother of Christ. *Please see Appendix C, "Mary's Family" for other thoughts of this nature.*

I think that Jesus portrays the spirit of our being able to access the OT notables when He was commenting to His disciples and the crowd about the faith of a Roman Centurion and He said:

> And I tell you this, that many Gentiles will come from all over the world – from east and west – and <u>sit down with Abraham, Isaac, and Jacob at the feast in the Kingdom of Heaven.</u> (Mat. 8:11 NLT)

---

1 Lacunza, Manuel, *The Coming of Messiah*, 326–7

2 Walvoord, John, *The Millennial Kingdom*, 325

3 *ibid.* 325

4 Truthnet.org, End times, *Armageddon and Christ's Return*, web

5 West, Nathaniel, *The Thousand Years in Both Testaments*, pp. 429–430

6 Pentecost, J. Dwight, *Things to Come*, 291

7 *ibid*, 291

8 *ibid*, 291

CHAPTER 7

PURPOSES AND BENEFITS OF THE MILLENNIUM

God has planned for this extraordinary era before the advent of mankind. He has laid out His grand scenario in which the thousand-year reign of Christ is its crown! I believe God has a number of purposes He intends to fulfill in Christ's Millennium and I also think there are some additional benefits which will also be experienced. Speakers and writers usually list half a dozen purposes for the Millennium; I list 23 purposes and 6 additional benefits.

PURPOSES

1. During this era, God will fulfill all of His covenants and promises to the Jews and their ancestors.
2. The Millennium will yield ". . . far more believers for eternity. How many will be alive at the end of the Millennium is total speculation. A guess of 10 times the current population of the Earth would not seem outrageous. Without the factors that decrease population, 60–70 billion might be conservative." [1]
3. This last dispensation will prove to angels and other heavenly creatures that one millennium of Christ's reign is infinitely superior to six millennia of Satan's.
4. The Millennium will show that obeying God's laws with Jesus as monarch over the entire earth produces the best societal results of all possible governments.

5. The Millennium will demonstrate that under Christ's guidance and protective governance, Christians outperform all others in acts beneficial to humanity and the causes of God.

6. This era will demonstrate that a Christ-controlled reign which employs the skills of Bride Saints, and mortal Christians and probably angels provides the closest environment to Heaven itself.

7. This time will verify that the evil Satan perpetrated, as the *ruler of the world,* was totally depraved, vicious and cruel (contributing to the eternal loss of countless souls [cf. Luke. 8:12]).

8. This will allow God to reward his saints (OT, NT and Tribulation) during his marvelous reign "with positions of authority over a millennial kingdom." [2]

9. The Millennium reestablishes and fulfills what God had originally intended for Adam and Eve and the planet, had they obeyed him.

10. The progressive revelation (concluding with the Millennium followed by the Satan-led rebellion) will prove conclusively that God was utterly just in judging and punishing Satan (and his angels). It will also demonstrate that He sacrificed greatly to allow Satan opportunity to try to prove he (and evil) should rule the universe and not God! *Please reference the Progressive Revelation, Appendix B for further information*

11. The Millennium (itself) fulfills numerous Bible prophecies. A very important example of that is Isaiah 9:6-7 which speaks of Jesus' reign in the Millennium.

12. God the Father fulfills His promises to Jesus (for

PURPOSES AND BENEFITS OF THE MILLENNIUM

example: John 6:37–39).

13. The Millennium provides the Sabbath proclaimed in Hebrews 4:9–11:

    So then, there remains a Sabbath rest for the people of God, for whoever has entered God's rest has also rested from his works as God did from his. Let us therefore strive to enter that rest . . . (Heb. 4:9–11a)

    The Millennium will constitute the Sabbath Rest. If the Day-Millennial Theory is correct, there will have been a week of *days*, each *day* consisting of 1000 years. It places the creation of Adam at 4000 years prior to Christ's first advent.

    Also, it places us on the cusp of the seventh day, that is, 2000 years since Jesus was *on earth*. Therefore, six millennial days have passed and the seventh (the Sabbath Rest) is about to begin. This theory is based on several concepts:

    a. The extensive use of the concept of a *week* (week of weeks, and of years) throughout Scripture. Examples are: the creation week, the 70 weeks of Daniel and the Feast of Weeks.

    b. The Scripture that says a thousand years is as a day to God and a day as a thousand years. (cf. 2 Pet. 3:8)

    c. The Day-Millennial theory is put forth in the Gospel of Barnabus (an apocryphal book).

    d. The current age of the earth as believed by young-earth proponents (6,000 to 10,000 years).

    e. The current age of mankind according to the Jewish calendar. Their calendar equivalent of 2012 is 5773.

f. The belief in the Millennial Day concept put forth in the Jewish Talmud.

14. Progressive Revelation will show that God's road to salvation is the only way; and that His overall plan of the ages is perfect.
15. Christ prepares His earthly Kingdom to present to God the Father at the conclusion of His reign (cf. 1 Cor. 15:24).
16. It will show that God was able to accomplish His plan for mankind (and especially Israel) despite all the evil efforts of Satan. He, as the god of this age (cf. 2 Cor. 4:4), has continuously schemed and worked to defeat the purpose and program of God.

    Satan tried repeatedly to annihilate <u>all Jews</u>. He consistently tortured and tempted Christians to sin and then (if they did) quickly slithered to God's throne to accuse them day and night (cf. Rev. 12:10).
17. All Jews will be saved (that is, the Tribulation remnant) and brought into the Millennial country of Israel. And so *all Israel* will be saved. As the Scriptures say, "The one who rescues will come from Jerusalem, and he will turn Israel away from ungodliness." (Rom. 11:26 NLT)
18. God will restore the original harmony between Himself and His creation, between what is supernatural and what is natural. In other words, redeem the earth from the curse.
19. It is necessary to manifest and exalt Christ in His resplendent glory as He rules with absolute power over His spectacular kingdom.
20. The Millennium provides the setting for the celebration

PURPOSES AND BENEFITS OF THE MILLENNIUM

of the Marriage of the Lamb and a kingdom over which Jesus and His Bride reign.

21. Jesus makes God's city, Jerusalem (and the land, Israel) the capital of the world.
22. Christ's reign allows His righteousness, truth and grace to emanate throughout the world.
23. The ultimate purpose is found in 1Corinthians 15:24–28, "that God may be all in all."

BENEFITS

This list of benefits derived from listing the purposes of the Millennium. It is necessarily incomplete but is meant to better define some qualities of this era.

1. All Millennial Christians are allowed to experience Christ's direct reign (and Bride Saints reigning with Him) prior to God's new Heaven and Earth.
2. Believers (immortal and mortal) who produced little fruit during their lifetime may be allowed to compensate during the Millennium. Our God is a God of second chances.
3. Christians (mortal and immortal) will be allowed to experience many of the ancient Israeli's temple rites.
4. All believers may be allowed to participate in the seven God-ordained feasts currently observed by orthodox Jews (in their fullest).
5. All immortal believers will experience how God works (and worked) to win people to himself.
6. Mankind will learn how to groom and utilize the earth as

BEYOND THE RAPTURE

God intended – how to wisely harvest its fruits, vegetables and other resources without damaging them.

---

1 Truthnet.org, End times, *Armageddon and Christ's Return*, web

2 *ibid.*

CHAPTER 8

WORSHIP IN JESUS' KINGDOM

Life during the Millennium will be exhilarating. It will center about the Lord Jesus. Joy and wonderment will echo throughout the earth. Worship will be spontaneous and deeply heartfelt with multitudes joining in loving agreement.

In the next two chapters, I cover a variety of topics to describe life for mortals during the Millennium. You will recall that believing mortals who survive the Tribulation and enter the Millennium will become the progenitors of myriads of mortal people. Whereas, those who enter the Millennium will be believers, their children will each have to decide for themselves. The various topics in these two chapters endeavor to describe the overall spiritual and then social environment that will exist by Christ's design, decree and enforcement. Every individual will be given the very best chance to decide in favor of Jesus. All indications are that Christ will harvest billions of believers for Himself during this time.

WORSHIP

The majority of Earth's inhabitants will follow Christ (at least during most of the Millennium).

> Nothing will hurt or destroy in all my holy mountain, for as the waters fill the sea, so the earth will be filled with people who know the Lord. (Isa. 11:9 NLT)

A great percentage of the families of earth will cultivate

Christianity within their families.

> They will speak of the glory of your kingdom; they will give examples of your power. They will tell about your mighty deeds and about the majesty and glory of your reign.
>
> For your kingdom is an everlasting kingdom. You rule throughout all generations. The Lord always keeps his promises; He is gracious in all he does. (Psa. 145:11–13 NLT)

MORTALS' RELATIONSHIP TO JESUS

Jesus will be worshipped worldwide. He will reign from Jerusalem however I believe His residence will be with His Bride in New Jerusalem (cf. Heb. 12:22-24).

Scripture establishes that both believing Israelis and Gentiles will enter Christ's temple (no non-believers allowed). So one might deduce that both rulers and commoners will make pilgrimages to Jerusalem. (cf. Psa. 72:11, 102:15)

There are many things the Bible does not tell us. Here are a few concepts that intrigue me.

In the Millennium, there will be the first valid and spontaneous emperor worship to ever occur. As Monarch of the Universe, will Jesus ever leave the areas of Israel or New Jerusalem? Would He ever visit the various nations of the earth?

Perhaps the answer to that question is that He will never again allow non-Christians into His presence. And therefore no non-Christians would ever see His face. This would rule out such visits to nations.

One very important concept not addressed is as follows:

WORSHIP IN JESUS' KINGDOM

Aside from worship services in every Gentile nation, how will individual mortals come to faith in Christ? That is, what will be the differences between faith in the Millennium versus faith in the church age?

- Faith will be by sight (i.e. mortals will receive a Messiah who is a visible and powerful reality).
- Resurrected believers will be present such that mortals will know their potential if they trust Christ.
- Satan and his deception and deterring force will be absent. Satan's evil system will be nonexistent. .
- The curse will be lifted so God's creation can be seen in its fullest beauty.
- Churches will be functioning at their greatest potential.
- The Holy Spirit will be providing a righteousness that is both palpable and irresistible. .
- Reports (or experiences) will exist of: God's Shekinah Glory,
- Christ's temple, the River of Life, the Trees of Life, a glorious Jerusalem and a resplendent Israel will be made available to mankind.
- There will be a history of the Rapture, the rescue and salvation of Israel, the resurrection of the OT and Tribulation Martyrs, the Coronation of Christ and the Marriage and Wedding Supper of the Lamb,

So then, how will the average Christian experience their Lord and Savior? They will know Him *in their hearts.*

They will know that He is reigning over the whole earth. But will they (in general) get to see Him in person before the establishment of the new Heaven and Earth? Due to the prevailing longevity of mortals, they might get to see Him a time or two. I pose this question in light of the billions of individuals who will come to live on the Millennial Earth (and the resultant logistics).

One mitigating factor will be the presence of the resurrected. Specifically, the Bride-saints will represent Christ to mortals (albeit in royal capacities).

I cannot imagine the amount of longing each mortal believer would have to meet Jesus personally (as do each of us at this time). For certain every Christian would vie for the opportunity to visit Jerusalem and their Lord. For all we know, they might try to outdo one another with tremendous good works to perchance gain sufficient accolades to earn a trip to visit Christ. I am speaking of believers who will live tremendous distances from Israel (e.g. in the area now occupied by China or USA).

The cross will still be emblematic of His reign (one of His signature icons). If He permits, pictures of Himself on His throne would grace the front of every church. Of course, Jesus could provide something resembling closed-circuit TV for every Christian assembly worldwide.

In California the original road between missions was named El Camino Real (The King's Highway). Perhaps every road to a church would be named in His honor.

> Set up road signs; put up guideposts.
> Mark well the path by which you came.
> Come back again, my virgin Israel;
> return to your towns here. (Jer. 31:21)

Throughout the world today, there are many monuments, statues and arches built to honor a variety of prominent individuals and events. It would be only natural

WORSHIP IN JESUS' KINGDOM

for people to want to do this for their wonderful Lord and Monarch.

THE CHURCH

Christianity will be the only *religion* known. *Gentile* worship services may be *designed* by Bride Saints to provide mortals the best opportunities to know and serve the Lord.

> The Lord will be king over all the earth. On that day there will be one Lord – his name alone will be worshiped. (Zec. 14:9)

Jesus might mandate church structure to be more like that of early church (as in Acts) where house churches were prevalent.

False religions and cults will not be permitted. Denominations within Christianity will probably no longer exist due to God-given clarity as to how Christians should function and believe. Probably the greatest difference will occur in approaches to evangelism, follow up and training in sanctification. Perhaps ethnicity and nationality will play a part as well.

Just as election was operative in both the NT and OT times (cf. Ephesians 1:4–5 and Daniel 12:1–2 respectively) and two thirds of all angels were elect to persevere, that is, not fall with Satan (cf. 1Timothy 5:21), so <u>election will probably be operative</u> during Christ's reign. And it appears the proportion of those saved will be significantly increased (maybe fifty to ninety percent will come to follow Jesus.)

Those who reject Christ will die by age 100 (cf. Isa. 65:20) and will be destined to perdition. Of course there are the millions who are seduced by Satan to attack God at Millennium's end (cf. Revelation 20:7–10). These facts (showing that a significant number reject Christ) are consistent with the election process. This is demonstrated by man's continued sinfulness and utter need to be drawn by God, despite God's overwhelming presence in the Millennium.

Evangelism will still be a necessary activity throughout society. Dominant among such activities will be the Jews who will send missionaries throughout the earth (cf. Isaiah 44:8, Jeremiah 16:19–21, Micah 5:5, Zechariah 8:21–23). They will be joined in this effort by all saints of the past and *present*. (cf. Isaiah 66:19)

The saints who rule earth (under Christ) might utilize the elders of every church (of the world) to provide the following:

- Connectivity to thoughts and desires of God. . . . . . .

- Teaching, correcting and mentoring their flocks in the ways of the Lord.

- Providing a greater knowledge of God than ever realized during OT times or the Church Age

Eldership in The Millennium will be far superior to that of the Church Age. Every quality designated as an elder requirement will be exhibited in excellence. Agape love will overflow and be contagious within the church and abound in the lives of the Millennial saints. Unfortunately too many elder boards have become problematic in our time. This trend will be delightfully reversed in The Millennium. With the influence of Christ's monarchy, the

WORSHIP IN JESUS' KINGDOM

Holy Spirit being so prevalent and Bride Saints in the ecclesiastical organization, churches will literally be aglow with the Spirit.

I would imagine that deacons would also be utilized in the churches. Their service will be a testimony to their church and neighborhood. They will not only serve church members but perform astounding acts of kindness and service to unbelievers in the power of Holy Spirit (in the spirit of Stephen, the first century martyr). Such things as these will be considered newsworthy in Christ's economy.

Aside: I believe that currently, pastors and elders hold positions of highest importance in our world; kings, presidents, prime ministers and dictators notwithstanding.

Likely the Jewish feast dates and sacrificial system will be observed in some way by Gentiles. The sacrificial system will in no way replace Christ's work on the cross, but rather commemorate His sacrifice graphically (especially since death will be relatively rare).

Only two Jewish feasts are mentioned with regard to the Millennium in the Old Testament, Tabernacles and Passover. So it could be that those are the only ones Christ desires. But it is possible that all seven Jewish feast dates would be observed. If so, they would not only commemorate God's love and past actions; but serve to remind and train Christians (and non-Christians) regarding aspects of God's love and program historically.

POTENTIAL CELEBRATION OF THE 7 FEAST DATES IN THE MILLENNIUM

NOTE: Scholars consider Christ as having fulfilled the first four of these feasts in His First Advent; and that the last three will be fulfilled during the beginning of His Second Advent. However, there is the caveat that, Jesus was probably born during the Feast of Tabernacles. *For reference purposes, the Feast Dates are ordained by God in Leviticus 23.*

1. Passover (Pesach)

   This is the first day of an eight day celebration commemorating the time when God protected the Jews from the Death Angel and released the Israelites from slavery in Egypt. During the Millennium we may:

   - Celebrate Christ's victory over sin and death for all believers.
   - Celebrate Christ's having rescued Israel at Tribulation's end.

2. Feast of Unleavened Bread

   Jews celebrated this feast the second day of Passover. This feast calls for a time of repentance and the putting away of sin. Leaven is symbolic of sin, so each Jewish home cleansed their home of leaven. During the Millennium we may:

   - Remember Christ's sinless body in death
   - Celebrate the resurrecteds' new sinless state. Jesus' righteousness has been imputed to us for all eternity.

3. First Fruits

   This feast coincides with the Harvest of Barley. The first sheaf from the winter sowing was offered priests in the Temple as unto the Lord. During the Millennium we may:

WORSHIP IN JESUS' KINGDOM

- Celebrate Jesus' resurrection (This will replace the somewhat faulty celebration of Easter [calendar-wise and name-wise]).
- Commemorate the Apostles lives and works

4. Feast of Weeks (Pentecost)

This feast is also a harvest Festival: The first fruits of the spring planting were brought to the temple as an offering. The feast also commemorated the giving of the Torah, The Law. During the Millennium we may:

- Celebrate The Holy Spirit's coming to earth to enable salvation and inaugurate Christ's church
- Commemorate the giving of The Law (some part of which will be in force)
- Celebrate the Sabbath rest of Christ (the Millennium)

5. Feast of Trumpets (Rosh Hashanah)

This fall feast was a sacred assembly called by Shofar. It marked God's giving the covenant of the Law to Israel. When God made this two-way covenant with them He showed His presence by smoke and fire atop Mt. Sinai.

The Feast of Trumpets begins the 10 days of awe in which the faithful prepare by being penitent in view of The Day of Atonement eight days later..During the Millennium we may:

- Celebrate the Rapture of the church (although it might have happened on a different day)
- Commemorate Christ's Second Advent

6. Day of Atonement (Yom Kippur)

This is a nation-wide feast for the intended cleansing of Israel's sins. During the Millennium we may:

- Remember the conversion of all the saints
- Celebrate our imputed righteousness (from Jesus to all believers)
- Feat Israel's national regeneration at Tribulation's end

7. Feast of Tabernacles (Booths)

This feast celebrates the fall harvest; it also commemorates the exodus and ensuing 40 years in the wilderness during which God sustained them. In the Millennium we may:

- Celebrate God's tabernacling with all the resurrected (and Israel) in New Jerusalem at beginning of Millennium and forever.
- Celebrate Christ's birth and life on earth; this instead of the poorly-timed and oft misguided observance of Christmas.

Yearly pilgrimages to Jerusalem will be commonplace.

> It shall come to pass in the latter days that the mountain of the house of the LORD shall be established as the highest of the mountains, and shall be lifted up above the hills; and all the nations shall flow to it, and many peoples shall come, and say: "Come, let us go up to the mountain of the LORD, to the house of the God of Jacob, that he may teach us his ways and that we may walk in his paths." For out of Zion shall go the law, and the word of the LORD from Jerusalem. (Isa. 2:2b–3)

The three festivals that were <u>pilgrimage festivals</u> during Jesus' first advent were Pentecost, Tabernacles and Passover. Each able-bodied male Jew was required to

WORSHIP IN JESUS' KINGDOM

journey to The Temple in Jerusalem. Orthodox Jews continue to observe these feasts today.

SABBATH ACTIVITIES

The Sabbath (either Saturday or Sunday) will be strictly observed and enforced. For believers, it will be an incredible daylong time of especially meaningful worship, (cf. Exo. 31:16)

Jesus may well proclaim (or communicate via Bride Saints) *Sermon on the Mount*-style sermons. Such would be more specific to the Millennial Age.

PROGRESSIVE REVELATION

Humans' behavior (and the Millennium overall) will provide the last of progressive revelation to the angelic host (with Satan and his abhorrent world system absent). "It is also to be God's final test of fallen humanity under the most ideal circumstances."[2] *Please reference Appendix B on Progressive Revelation.*

In Scripture, we are told that temptation comes from the world, the flesh and the devil. In the Millennium, only the flesh *remains* and that alone will require Jesus to reign with a *fist of iron*. Righteousness will reign but not without rebellion and heartache.

RIGHTEOUSNESS ENFORCED

Mortals will still have a sin nature and will need to accept Jesus as Savior to experience true worship. Humans may have 100 years to accept Christ (or suffer death).

> Never again will there be in it an infant who lives but a few days, or an old man who does not live out his years; the one who dies at a hundred will be thought a mere child; the <u>one who fails to reach a hundred will be considered accursed.</u> (Isa. 65:20 NIV)

On an even more severe note, all "will be subject to Christ's reign and if openly rebellious will be put to death. (cf. Isa. 66:24)."[3]

> All humanity will come to worship me from week to week and from month to month. And as they go out, they will see the dead bodies of those who have rebelled against me. (Isa. 66:23–24 NLT)

God shows His intolerance of rebellious nations throughout Psalm 2 which speaks pointedly about Christ's reign.

Christ's "government will be absolute in its authority and power. This is demonstrated in His destruction of all who oppose Him. (cf. Psa. 2:9, 72:9–11; Isa. 11:4)"[4]

> But with righteousness he shall judge the poor, and decide with equity for the meek of the earth; and he shall strike the earth with the rod of his mouth, and with the breath of his lips he shall kill the wicked. (Isa. 11:4)

THE HOLY SPIRIT

Offsetting this sobering prospect is the magnificent ministry of the Holy Spirit during the Millennium.

"The remarkable, astounding outpouring of the Holy Spirit as presented in the Millennial descriptions...so powerful in *His* transforming, glorifying and imparting miraculous gifts to the saints; so pervading in and over the Jewish nation that all shall be righteous from the least to the greatest; so wide-reaching over the Gentiles that they shall rejoice in the light bestowed. ... The magnificent portrayals of the Millennial and succeeding ages are so sublime with the indwelling, abiding, communicated Divine, that no one can contemplate it, without being profoundly moved at the display of spirituality."[5]

"It is evident from the Scriptures that all believers will be indwelt by the Holy Spirit ... even as they are in the present age. (Ezekiel 36:27, 37:14, Jer. 31:33)"[6]

"The filling of the Holy Spirit will be common in the Millennium, in contrast to the infrequency of it in other ages, and it will be manifested in worship and praise of the Lord and in willing obedience to Him as well as in spiritual power and inner transformation. (cf. Isa. 32:15; 44:3 Ezk. 39:29, Joel 2:28–29)"[7]

"The joy of the Lord will pervade the earth. A significant portion of all humanity will become Christian. God's righteousness will be pervasive."[8]

Christians (mortal) will probably not die. With the curse removed, life spans could equal that of Methuselah who lived until age 969. (cf. Isa. 65:20, 22c)

RITUALS

There will probably be new Christian rituals in the Millennium. Some might derive from the OT Temple ceremonies and Jewish religious observances (for example: Passover Seders). But at least three should carry over from New Testament times, namely communion, marriage and baptism.

. During communion, we will remember Christ's supreme sacrifice (His Passion) with a fervor and appreciation far surpassing any previously experienced. Because Jesus becomes a wonderful *present reality*, communion will translate into ecstatic worship of our triumphant and heroic King. That we will partake of communion is strongly indicated herein:

> I tell you, I will not drink from this fruit of the vine from now on until that day when I drink it new with you in my Father's kingdom." (Mat: 26:29 NIV)

I suspect marriage (at least marriage in Israel) will revert to the Jewish style wedding as described in Appendix E Ancient Jewish Weddings Practices. However it is ritualized, it will usually be celebrated with great spiritual emphasis.

Baptism will be similar in nature and purpose to what we now know but will probably be far more glorious. First of all, the Bride and OT saints would probably prevent any tares from being baptized. Such would not be necessarily forever condemned but probably would be mentored by someone until they had truly received Jesus as Lord and Savior.

The dimensionality which could be added (to baptism) would be far more meaningful festivities and celebration (sponsored by all Bride and OT saints who were privy to the conversion process [of those being baptized]). In addition, Bride and OT saints might convey special messages from Jesus Himself.

WORSHIP IN JESUS' KINGDOM

<u>MUSIC</u>

Music in The Millennium will be incredible. There will be an ever-increasing amount of different instruments, virtuosity and composition.

In the revival of the 70s, many Christian songs were composed. In the Millennium, as we get to know Jesus intimately, we will compose greater, grander songs and hymns. In a wonderful new dimension, our Triune God may create songs and sing to us or have us sing them (or both).

My wife's (Helen) mental picture of such was God's wondrous music coming from an area of dazzling white with a mammoth set of many curving stairs surrounded by golden hues. The scenes described in Revelation 4 and 5 inspired these thoughts.

1 WikiAnswers web
2 Pentecost, 477
3 Walvoord, 302
4 *ibid.* 301
5 Peters, op. cit., III, *The Theocratic Kingdom*, 465
6. John F. Walvoord, *The Holy Spirit*, pp 233–234
7. *ibid.* pp 233–234
8 Pentecost, 488

CHAPTER 9

LIFE IN CHRIST'S KINGDOM

In this chapter we will consider what day-to-day life might be like under the wonderful reign of Christ.

MORTALS

The curse will have been lifted – that will make life much easier for mortals. However, their sin nature will still daunt them.

With people transitioning to The Millennium from the Tribulation, what memories, wounds and disabilities (mental, physical and emotional) would they naturally carry with them? So Christ will intervene, such that Tribulation saints will probably not suffer crippling aftereffects from having lived through this horrific era (cf. Isa. 35:5–6).

Another consideration is the longevity of the Tribulation Survivor saints (living as mortals in The Millennium). Whereas those born into The Millennium would have long-life bodies like Methuselah (cf. Isa. 65:20, 22); those coming from the Tribulation would have current-earth bodies.

So whether or not Jesus would *retrofit* these people with long-life bodies is a matter of conjecture. Another possibility is that these people would have to move close to the River of Life to be able to receive its life-sustaining help. (review Chapter 4, Christ's Kingdom, The Temple). Were they or any others in the Millennium subject to death, then one might expect them to be resurrected near the time of the Great White Throne Judgment. Both believers and non-believers who die during The Millennium would necessarily be resurrected. Believers might have a Bema Seat judgment after receiving their immortal bodies. Non-believers would stand before the Great White Throne judgment seat.

Millennial humans will go about life in much the same way as we do today. However, I feel normative society would have to be reestablished (at the beginning) as Jesus distributes mortals around the world in settlements. Once placed, everyone might have to act as pioneers and *carve out* their own niche.

Jesus will cause the earth to be far more productive such that fruit trees and other natural food sources would be easy to cultivate.

"The time will come," says the Lord, "when the grain and grapes will grow faster than they can be harvested. Then the terraced vineyards on the hills of Israel will drip with sweet wine!" (Amos 9:13)

POPULATION

Mortals will still marry, reproduce and have large families. Earth's population will *explode.* I have done a calculation of how many people might exist by the Millennium's end. I used a very conservative beginning figure of 100,000 mortals entering the Millennium.

Estimating that each family would have at least two children, I calculated earth's population as doubling every fifty years. The figure that results is about 100 billion people. If only half of them became believers, that would leave 50 billion Christians at Millennium's end. That is a staggering thought is it not? What a harvest for the Lord!

Using the same formula and starting with one million people would yield one trillion; starting with one billion would yield a quadrillion. Such figures are mind-boggling and leave us scratching our collective heads as to whether that is even possible.

As difficult as this is to comprehend, here's one possibility that escaped me until I investigated. Consider the following quote from WikiAnswers:

"29% of Earth is land mass. Of that land mass, humans occupy less than 1%.. Of the remaining 28% about 40% is pure wilderness. 14% is true desert and 15% has desert like characteristics. 9% is Antarctica. Most of the remaining 22% are agricultural areas."[1]

I would suggest that Jesus could (and would) easily render much more of earth as habitable.

GOVERNMENT

Jesus will be the reigning monarch of the world. In the previous world there had been faulty and evil emperor worship (e.g. the Caesars). In the Millennium, the *emperor* worship of our Lord and Savior will be spontaneous and more than appropriate. His will be a monarchy (or theocracy) which is marvelous and matchless.

For Jesus to be both emperor and the object of worship will evoke an attitude of total cooperation with governing authorities; and this phenomena will extend worldwide. Such obedience will be furthered by the salvation and godliness of the majority; righteousness will be very pervasive. Even as we consider such a society we are hard put to conceptualize it. No Christians, much less the world, have experienced anything approaching such a society. Yes we have had godly leaders but none we could worship. Yes we have worshipped Jesus but never as a present reigning monarch. To have Jesus as our reigning Emperor can only be joyously imagined yet in a totally inadequate fashion.

Spiritual and civil obedience during the Millennium can evolve two primary ways. Ideally those being sanctified are obeying Christ, becoming increasingly godly and therefore genuinely and honestly supporting government.

On the other hand, salvation may come later in life to some. These non-Christians will struggle with their sin natures and some will rebel against the *law of the land*. Sadly they might rail against our Emperor Himself. This is the primary reason ruling authorities must keep crime (and to lesser degree sin) in check. Rather like how the priests and rulers of Israel enforced the Law of Moses and the Levitical laws which accompanied them, Christ's government working hand in hand with His Church will oversee all of human life on earth.

The abundance of the Fruit of The Spirit will demonstrate Christ's power in love. Sinfulness and unrepentance will be met not with harshness but with loving correction and firmness. God's love demonstrated by the many will foster salvation. This prevailing environment should bring godly conviction at several levels: internally, interpersonally, societally and from righteous government.

The love abounding from our King of Kings and then amongst believers will be overwhelming. Christ's

LIFE IN CHRIST'S KINGDOM

wonderful priestly and kingly governance is a primary reason my original book is titled, *Christ's Spectacular Millennium*.

GOD'S BELOVED ISRAEL

In Jesus' monarchy, Israel will be His beloved country and Jerusalem His crown jewel.

> In the last days, the mountain on which the Lord's Temple stands will become the most important of all mountains. It will be raised above the hills, and people from all nations will come streaming to it. (Isa. 2:2)

> Be glad and rejoice forever in that which I create; for behold, I create Jerusalem to be a joy, and her people to be a gladness. I will rejoice in Jerusalem and be glad in my people; no more shall be heard in it the sound of weeping and the cry of distress (Isa. 65:18–19)

The Apostles received a special promise from Jesus:

> You have stayed with me in my time of trial. And just as my Father has granted me a Kingdom, I now grant you the right to eat and drink at my table in my Kingdom. And you will sit on thrones, judging the twelve tribes of Israel. (Luke 22:28–30 NLT)

David may rule Jerusalem. (cf. Jer. 30:9) "There are a number of references which establish the regency of David in the Millennium." [2] This is never stated explicitly but because Jesus is never called David, and in a number of Millennial passages, the Prince is referred to as 'My servant David,' theologians deduce that David shall rule (but in a subservient way to Christ). The 12 apostles will rule the tribes of Israel. (cf. Luke. 22:30). Palestine will be redistributed among the 12 tribes of Israel. (cf. Ezk. 48:1–29)[3]

BEYOND THE RAPTURE

In that day, Israel, your cities will be rebuilt, and your borders will be extended. People from many lands will come and honor you from Assyria all the way to the towns of Egypt, from Egypt all the way to the Euphrates River, and from distant seas and mountains. (Mic. 7:11–12 NLT)

Not only will Israel be greatly expanded as a nation but the countries which subjugated her (prior to the 21st century) will now be subjugated to her: Egypt, Assyria, Persia, Babylon and Rome (Italy).

They will take captive those who were their captors, and rule over those who oppressed them. (Isa. 14:2c)

This leaves the fate of a number of countries open for speculation. Germany and Russia murdered millions of Jews during and just after World War II. Only a minor investigation into European countries complicit for their cooperation with the Nazis yields dismaying results. Far too many were unbelievably cooperative in the extermination of the Jews. For certain, Jesus will judge them accordingly; so I should think Russia and Germany would only be the starting point for those European countries who will be subjugated to Israel. What might this mean? The prophet Isaiah declares that Christ would permit Israel to establish rulership of these countries. They would be recipients of the spoils of same. That is, Israel would receive choice goods, products and produce. The people of said countries would serve Israel and its people however Israel's leadership desired.

PAX CHRISTUS

Honest, effective government will be a hallmark of Christ's reign. Those entering Christ's Millennium will be increasingly astounded by the lack of self-serving

LIFE IN CHRIST'S KINGDOM

politicians and the presence of a loving, just government. The Kingdom will be characterized by truth (in contrast with the Soviet Union [and other communist countries], where *the lie* was so prevalent).

> May God be gracious to us and bless us and make his face to shine upon us, that your way may be known on earth, your saving power among all nations. Let the nations be glad and sing for joy, for you judge the peoples with equity and guide the nations upon earth. (Psa. 67:1–3a,)

> Let the peoples praise you, O God; the earth has yielded its increase; God, our God, shall bless us. God shall bless us; let all the ends of the earth fear him! (Psa. 67:5–7)

Jesus implies that there will be a hierarchical government. In the Parable of the Talents (cf. Luke 19:11–27), the master awards the diligence of two of the slaves with governorship over multiple cities. From this I infer that there will be the equivalence of today's towns, cities, counties, states, regions and countries (or some variation thereof). Also, the angels of God have titles which imply hierarchical government: Archangels, Seraphim and Cherubim. These titles suggest differing roles, rank and responsibilities.

The following verses also imply structured government (in the angelic realm).

> For by him (Jesus) all things were created, in Heaven and on earth, visible and invisible, whether thrones or dominions or rulers or authorities – all things were created through him and for him. (Col. 1:16)

Because the government will be a godly theocracy, it will require total interaction between governing authorities and Christ's priesthood (all Bride Saints). These priests will provide a liaison to the masses, teaching them Jesus' societal rules and requirements. The laws will be made known to people through a permanent and binding catechism which perfectly reflects Christ's desires and His Word.

"Because of the presence of Messiah, Jerusalem shall be the source from which all millennial righteousness will emanate in dazzling glory. (cf. Isa. 61:11)" [4]

The official world language will be Hebrew (at least for the purposes of worship and diplomacy).

> Then I will purify the speech of all people, so that everyone can worship the Lord together. (Zep. 3:9)

Whereas the perfection of this theocracy will be magnificent, it will be the very thing that the rebellious will revile and challenge. Such will be met and deterred by the loving, infinitely wise priests and ruling authorities.

With the ever-burgeoning populace, strict enforcement will be a necessity to maintain a near-perfect society.

Nations (except Israel), states, cites, and villages will all be headed in some way by kings as well as Bride and Tribulation Saints. The resurrected will assure that godliness prevails (no corruption as with current day politicians worldwide. [cf. Rev. 20:6]) *You may reference Appendix H "A Theoretical Governmental Model" to read my suppositions about how it might happen.* (Take note that the Bible does not spell it out.)

There will be little weaponry and that no more advanced than in ancient days. I would not expect guns to be in the mix.

> And I will make for them a covenant on that day ... and I will abolish the bow, the sword, and war from the land, and I will

LIFE IN CHRIST'S KINGDOM

make you lie down in safety. (Hos. 2:18)

They shall beat their swords into plowshares, and their spears into pruning hooks; nation shall not lift up sword against nation, neither shall they learn war anymore (Isa. 2:4c)

"The government will deal summarily with any outbreak of sin." [5]

Crimes will still be committed however:

- All law enforcement will be buttressed by Bride Saints (angels may be *the police* or aid us in identifying and locating perpetrators).
- Justice will be swift and appropriate.
- All criminals will be caught quickly.
- Every inhabitant on earth will receive perfect justice.
- Criminality will be held in check in that no crime will go undetected or unpunished.
- The wealthy will not be allowed to oppress the poor.
- I would expect an *eye for an eye* type of punishment. Also, I believe restitution would be required for damage and theft. Note that restitution has proven an effective deterrent to recidivism in today's society.

Of the increase of his government and of peace there will be no end, on the throne of David and over his kingdom, to establish it and to uphold it with justice and with righteousness from this time forth and forevermore. The zeal of the LORD of hosts will do this. (Isa. 9:7)

People should have a voice in local government but not regarding morality or behavior.

I believe that many of the Levitical laws regarding social (not necessarily religious) behavior will be in force.

BEYOND THE RAPTURE

This will produce a Judeo-Christian ethic infinitely superior to that which was in place in the USA until the 1960's. In the next few paragraphs I will state my reasoning.

Jesus will rule with a *rod of iron*. Therefore it is quite reasonable that He will not countenance activity contrary to His righteous requirements. I believe the basic criminal laws which are enforced in USA would (for the most part) be pleasing and required by Him. Unfortunately, the Judeo-Christian laws that existed for two hundred years in USA regarding immoral sexual behavior have been set aside in recent decades, for example: regarding homosexuality. I think these will be reinstituted.

Gone will be the maniacal, murderous dictatorships and false religions; forgotten the genocides with the demonic forces dispensing destruction and misery. Totally eclipsing all this satanic mayhem will be God's love, joy, peace and freedom worldwide emanating from the Lord of Lord and King of Kings.

MORALITY

In the Millennium, decency laws will be in force and enforced. In USA, prior to the *Supreme* Court (sic) overruling such in the 1960s, the FCC monitored all radio and TV broadcasts. Anything of a vulgar or seditious nature was literally zapped, and the guilty were fined. I can remember TV shows halting abruptly after some obscene comment or act occurred (back in the 50s).

Under Christ's reign, the ability to commit unrighteous acts publically would be prohibited. Gambling and the public dispensing of alcohol and recreational drugs would be curtailed. Commercial prostitution (such as Nevada

LIFE IN CHRIST'S KINGDOM

permits) would not be allowed. Unnatural sex acts would be considered criminal. If movies and TV are permitted, only that which is morally healthy would be allowed. To put it succinctly, all things flagrantly sinful would be illegal and precluded. Instead, people would learn to do and enjoy those activities which are morally healthy and desirable.

Laws regarding banking, commerce, employment and society in general would be established in such a way that truth and legitimacy would be strictly required. The question which cannot be answered at this time is, "How severe will the penalties be?" Will there be "an eye for an eye and a tooth for a tooth" type of laws? Will the death penalty be applicable to as many illegal or immoral infractions as it was under the Mosaic system of law?

For certain the burgeoning mortal populous, which still will have a sin nature, will require tough regulation. In the Roman Empire, the Pax Romano (Roman peace) was enforced, quite brutally at times. In the Millennium, a *Pax Christus* (Christ's Peace) will be enforced. This will require strict enforcement at personal, city, state and national levels.

Thus mortals will be subject to Christ's laws. Although life could be entirely idyllic, sin will plague each person. That will be manifested in their tendency to *get into trouble*. Promiscuity and debauchery will still arise within people. Some will resent the enforcement of the Judeo/Christian ethic. However the overall qualities and pervasiveness of the Millennial reign will do much to counteract this. Spiritually healthy families will be abundant and will provide a good springboard for each youth.

BEYOND THE RAPTURE

SOCIETY

Earth may have agrarian settings similar to the Amish today. In other words, like God designed it to be originally. Modern mechanical devices, computers et al may not exist.

"So I will gather all nations and peoples together, and they will see my glory. ... They will bring the remnant of your people back from every nation. They will bring them to my holy mountain in Jerusalem as an offering to the Lord. <u>They will ride on horses, in chariots and wagons, and on mules and camels,</u>" says the Lord. (Isa. 66:18c–20)

The simple, peaceful life I describe may not be the case. Perhaps many of the inventions (modernization) of premillennial Earth will be incorporated.

A question to ponder is, "Are we doing disservice to God to think He would quash many of the human inventions from the past several millennia?"

It is quite possible that many of humanity's positive accomplishments may be retained. Cultural masterpieces, medical treatments, and technological advancements may be things that Jesus would choose to allow into His Kingdom.

Although the Great Tribulation would have wiped out most of current earth's modern conveniences, it might not obliterate memory of such. Certain skills and crafts should be remembered by Survivor mortal saints.

How many of our mechanized vehicles will be retained or restored – bicycles, autos or aircraft? We ponder, why not – what harm would it do? God will have decided how much mortals can automate or modernize without encouraging more sinfulness or opposing the way He wishes mortals to function. Whatever the case, the populace will be able to work their respective trades successfully and prosper.

HUMANITY

Family life will be pleasant, divorce rare. Parents will be respected and obeyed. In turn, parents will honor and groom their children for life, especially to lead exemplary Christian lives.

Friendship and love will be prevalent. Godly life will be a pervasive quality worldwide. There will be far more philanthropy due to Millennium mores and family training and ties.

Life for mortals will be wonderful from birth onward. Gone will be wars, conflicts, and blatantly criminal activity. Due to the righteousness typical of the majority, personal abuses will be at a minimum. Marriage would be the goal of most youth and it would be held in highest esteem. The Christian influence in most marriages would provide strong modeling.

Youth would be educated about marital relationships and especially about parenting. They would be taught how to guide their children into relationships and vocations. These youth would be able to *practice* as they related to their younger siblings and their friends. This would cause them to understand the goals and actions of their own parents. Respect and love would be tantamount in all training, guidance and development. All training would be tied into the Christian catechism and curriculum.

Because believing mortals may not die (or at least live

hundreds of years) tremendous family trees will be forged. Each original couple will become Christian patriarchs with scores of generations and thousands in their family. An interesting question will be, "At what age will they stop having children themselves?"

I believe that people will retain their ethnicity and color in the Millennium. (cf. Rev. 5:9). I also infer this from the mention of nations, tribes, etcetera in the following verse:

> After this I saw a vast crowd, too great to count, from every nation and tribe and people and language, standing in front of the throne and before the Lamb. They were clothed in white robes and held palm branches in their hands. (Rev. 7:9)

ANIMALS

Wild animals will not fear Bride Saints and probably not mortals either. God had informed Noah:

> Every animal on earth, every bird in the sky, every animal that crawls on the ground, and every fish in the sea will respect and fear you. I have given them to you. (Gen. 9:2)

This fear seems to have continued throughout earth's history. But in the Millennium, wild animals will no longer be a threat to mortals (cf. Hos. 2:18, Rev. 19:14). They will also be far less wary of humans and probably tamable.

> In that day the wolf and the lamb will live together; the leopard will lie down with the baby goat. The calf and the yearling will be safe with the lion, and a little child will lead them all. The cow will graze near the bear. The cub and the calf will lie down together. The lion will eat hay like a cow. The baby will play safely near the hole of a cobra. Yes, a little child will put its hand in a nest of deadly snakes without harm. (Isa. 11:6–8 NLT)

LIFE IN CHRIST'S KINGDOM

When such statements are made *about the lion and the lamb* plus *the child and the snake*, huge changes to the world's animal kingdom are implied. In these short quotes, God's changing the anatomical design of hundreds (if not thousands) of creatures bodies is necessitated. With these simple statements, we are also shown the vast and devastating alterations imposed on the animal kingdom when Adam and Eve's world was cursed by God.

Both wild and tame animals will obey OT and Bride Saints. The resurrected should be able to communicate with all animals. An interesting preview of this is Monty Robert's equinus language, by which he is able to communicate with and control horses (both wild and domesticated). He can train them to be ridden far more humanely (and much faster) than with the brutal techniques traditionally utilized. His equinus language is also effective with deer.

I am an animal lover and have enjoyed swimming with dolphins and petting various wild animal youngsters. I love to watch people work with raptors such as eagles and owls. I believe we will be able to have *up close and personal* encounters with any animals we desire. Bride Saints may well have dominion over them.

Indications are that horses will be prevalent again.

On that day even the harness bells of the horses will be inscribed with these words: Holy to the Lord. (Rev. 14:20)

There will probably be myriads of choices for pets. Personally, my first choice for pets would be my pets from the past but I do not know if that will be possible. As far as exotic animals, I want panda cubs (to cuddle), a silver-back gorilla and beautiful male lion for pets. Such fantasy!

BEYOND THE RAPTURE

A curiosity question is whether Christ will restore flora or fauna that have gone extinct; (e.g. dinosaurs and flying reptiles)?

VOCATIONS

Jobs could revert to the simpler trades, for example: tailoring, baking, blacksmithing, clerking, ranching, farming, etcetera. It will all depend on how much technology is permitted or needed. Much of today's technology is geared towards making life easier and more convenient. With the earth's curse lifted and the abundance of food, need for certain technologies will abate. A significant part of today's technology is geared for war and defense. There will be no such industry. So as one ticks through the various technologies, it becomes apparent certain ones would no longer be required or desired.

Overall it could be more of a natural, agrarian-based society. Farming will be easy and natural. Vegetables and fruit will be abundant. Again, we simply cannot project many aspects of the Millennium.

EDUCATION

Beyond elementary school, apprenticeships will once again be the common way to train young people. This is not to say there will not be higher education.

Elementary school will include training in Christianity (with some form of catechism).

Gone will be the myriads of misinformed and misinforming instructors (who existed at every level of schooling before the Second Advent). Youth, instead, will be steeped in God's truth by strong Christian teachers. Gone will be all destructive and deluding philosophy, religion and paradigms. God's freedom, truth, love and peace will reign worldwide - ever cleansing, renewing and invigorating individuals, peoples and nations.

The Bible would be prevalent in all matters. It will be interesting to see if God will update it to include the account of the Tribulation and establishment of the Millennium. Perhaps a God-given book of accurate church history might be introduced. Such could be created for use in the New Earth. One strong argument for this happening is that any born during the Millennium would have no idea of the arduous life for most Christians on earth preceding the Millennium. Folk lore or word of mouth would be all they would have to rely upon unless they were informed in some way by God and/or the Immortals (NT, OT and Tribulation Saints). Even today we have but meager information about the early church and overall church history. Having such a history in the Millennium would certainly glorify God and serve as a warning about Satan and his demons.

Likely, prominent notables of both Old Testament and New Testament times will be in demand to share their wisdom and their testimonies.

SCIENCE

Using the *why not* approach, it seems the sciences would be studied and utilized in the Millennium. Gone would be the greatest hindrance to scientific development in our day, namely the theory of evolution.

I believe the resurrected would have great inherent

understanding of things scientific by virtue of their improved minds and standing with Christ. Whether we would share our *secrets* with mortals remains to be seen.

How advanced Jesus would permit mortals to become is unspecified and unknown. One thing that comes to mind with this regard is that so many of our modern inventions, though marvelous in ways are also employed for evil. For instance, too much of internet traffic has been dedicated to pornography. Criminals and terrorists use it to facilitate their crimes.

I am reminded of the story of Alfred Nobel, the Swedish chemist. He was the inventor of dynamite. His rationale and focus was to assist with a variety of construction needs. However, its use in weaponry greatly disturbed and haunted Mr. Nobel. He did not want to be remembered as dynamite's inventor so he instituted the concept of the Nobel Prize (using his vast wealth). And that is how most people remember him.

With that said, I feel Jesus may very well limit certain scientific advancement to help mitigate the evil that mortals might do.

On the other hand, if He permitted or even encouraged the sciences, the heights to which knowledge could rise would far surpass anything we have yet known. God would bring to light truths and phenomena glorifying and pointing to God (things that Satan had terribly obscured).

ENTERTAINMENT

I believe vacations will be commonplace but the type of transportation venues that might be available (primitive or sophisticated) would depend on the answers to the previous questions about technical advancement.

Use of hard liquor and recreational drugs will not be allowed. Counteracting this will be the fact that the joy of the Lord will be quite prevalent and life will be so wonderful. Therefore, there will be so much less motivation to partake of such mind altering substances. With such a blessed society, which is loving, fair and righteous, the need or desire for *getting high* would be far less. Food, employment, housing and most every basic requirement for living comfortably will be readily available in Christ's kingdom worldwide. These Edenic conditions will make suffering and misery minimal.

The news of today focuses largely on that which is lurid, tragic or criminal: theft, murder, rape and other crimes (such as those sins described in Galatians 5:19–21). Another focus is the rich and famous. By contrast, the focus during the Millennium will be topics such as: spiritual gains, heroes of faith, and great examples of gifts and fruit of the Spirit. Myriad acts of kindness of God, the Bride and OT saints will be *hot topics.* But how and to what extent will news be disseminated?

Of course social, political and local happenings would be reported (but with a healthy focus). Messages might come from our Triune God as well. *They* might keep us informed of all that is being accomplished for God's kingdom throughout the world (from *their* perspective).

Movies, TV and the like probably will not exist as we know them. Instead of TV et al, there could be story times in which OT and Tribulation saints glorify God by sharing His awesome acts on their behalf on earth. Such stories could be illustrated with God-provided 3-D capabilities (unknown holographics which far eclipse current earth capabilities).

Plays, games, sports and parties will probably be standard venue. The arts will be prevalent in all societies.

God might supernaturally re-create elaborate scenes from the Old Testament for the Bride and Old Testament saints (and perhaps mortals).

BIRTHDAYS

Perhaps each Christian will celebrate his birthday as the historical day he (or she) became a believer. Celebration of this day will be quite different from birthdays now. I will let you imagine how you would celebrate your spiritual birthday.

Now let me add to your thoughts. We could relate our personal testimony. In the case of Bride Saints, our personal angel might show up to demonstrate how he (and other angels) celebrated our conversion.

> Just so, I tell you, "There is joy before the angels of God over one sinner who repents." (Luke 15:10)

Then we could ask our angel to explain (or provide visuals of) what all was going on in the unseen spiritual world around us, accompanying our conversion. He might tell or show how the angels battled for our very souls.

> The angel of the LORD encamps around those who fear him, and delivers them. (Psa. 34:7)

> For we do not wrestle against flesh and blood, but against the rulers, against the authorities, against the cosmic powers over this present darkness, against the spiritual

LIFE IN CHRIST'S KINGDOM

forces of evil in the heavenly places. (Eph 6:12)

Also reference Isaiah 63:9 (NIV) and 2Kings 6:15–17 regarding angelic activity.

God or your angel could invite/bring all those contributing to your salvation to the party – those who prayed for you, witnessed to you, and led you to Christ.

HEALTH

Whether resurrected or translated, Bride Saints will have new bodies. The diseased will be made whole. The lame or maimed will be fully functional. The once blind will see perfectly. The previously deaf will hear with perfect clarity (cf. Isa. 29:18). Disease, deformities and dysfunction will be nonexistent.

For Millennial mortals, good health will prevail in Christ's utopian environment. Accidents, some births and other situations will still require a doctor's care. Vaccinations will probably not be needed. Holistic remedies and treatments for minor ailments will be widely known and utilized.

The River of Life (cf. Rev. 22:1) and the trees with Leaves of Healing (cf. Rev 22:2) will undoubtedly play a significant part in the overall health of the world.

WEATHER

Weather would undoubtedly be far tamer than what we experience these days. Tornadoes, hurricanes, blizzards, hail storms and earthquakes would be less frequent if not rare.

BEYOND THE RAPTURE

However, as Christ rules, He will withhold rain from misbehaving nations or punish them with damaging weather.

Any nation in the world that refuses to come to Jerusalem to worship the King, the Lord of Heaven's Armies, will have no rain. (Zec. 14:17 NLT)

Then the Lord will provide shade for Mount Zion and all who assemble there. He will provide a canopy of cloud during the day and smoke and flaming fire at night covering the glorious land. It will be a shelter from daytime heat and a hiding place from storms and rain. (Isa. 4:5–6)

---

1 WikiAnswers, Net

2 Pentecost, *Things to Come,* 498

3 ibid. 510

4 ibid. 483

5 ibid. 501

CHAPTER 10

FINAL EVENTS

Let us now examine the events that conclude the Millennium. I will touch on when and why Satan is loosed; and what Christ might do to protect the Christians and the Resurrected during that time. What will the Great White Throne Judgment be and mean to us? Finally we will explore what happens to the Millennial Kingdom as God dispenses with the heavens and earth and then re-creates them.

As life in The Millennium progresses through time, the population will *explode*. With no synthetic birth control and limited death, the population will gain rapidly but Christ will have prepared the earth for just such a scenario. More and more Bride and OT saints will be *employed* to govern and direct. This would probably be true of the angelic population as well; that is, utilized to assist Christ and the resurrected govern earth.

END OF THE MILLENIUM

Many of the dynamics and qualities of life will evolve as the Millennium *ages*. There will be countless people from infants to *super-seniors* 800 to 900 years old. Bride and OT Saints will be overseeing greater and greater hierarchies of churches, administrations and kingdoms. Knowledge and capabilities at both spiritual and secular levels will reach heights unimaginable. Christ's Kingdom will peak just as He planned. Perhaps in the Millennial era's final years, Christ will escalate efforts to win the lost. He may desire Bride Saints and OT Saints to participate.

It might happen this way: angelic host would precede us declaring God's glory and salvation as they hovered over mankind (cf. Rev.14:6–7). Then God could direct a special orbit of New Jerusalem. From this vantage point, we would be directed to descend on specific areas to proclaim God's love with an urgency to accept that love and grace. Through the ministry of the Holy Spirit, many will give their lives to Christ, yet sadly a large number will remain in rebellion.

In Chapter 8 in the section *Mortals' Relationship to Jesus,* I listed nine marvelous situations and/or qualities of the Millennium that would enhance God's witness. These would greatly help to evangelize the lost. I feel the greatest of these nine qualities is:

- Faith will be by sight (i.e. mortals will receive a Messiah who is a visible and powerful reality).
- Resurrected believers will be present such that mortals will know their potential if they trust Christ.
- The Holy Spirit will be providing a righteousness that is both palpable and irresistible.

Though these witnesses far exceed anything we had experienced on earth during Christ's First Advent or the Church Age, yet mankind's innate sinfulness will be still be present and become painfully exposed. This rebellion is incomprehensible in light of Jesus' beautiful and paradisiacal Millennium; such conditions would have reverberating impact spiritually, physically and emotionally.

FINAL EVENTS

Yet all we need do is to recall how (in the Gospels) the Jewish leaders would witness one after another of Jesus' miracles and then desire to put Him to death (cf. Mat. 12:14, John 4:53 and 5:18). As a matter of fact, after Jesus raised Lazarus from the dead, they wanted to put Lazarus to death! (cf. John 12:10). Such responses are hideous and unfathomable to us believers. And we see Jewry down through history suffering as a result of their rebellion, their depravity and spiritual blindness.

So counter to all our righteous logic, there will be millions susceptible to Satan's upcoming plot and accompanying seduction to overthrow God from ruling over them. At that time, there will be millions of people under the age of 100. Unfortunately, many will be undecided or rebellious about following Jesus. Once loosed, Satan will pounce upon them and entice many of them to join him in an attempt to overthrow Christ. He will demonstrate his power (present and past) to deceive. His powers of deception are so ingrained that he deceives himself into thinking he can overpower God.

Christ will have precluded anything resembling war until the Millennium has ended. Then He will take action to separate remaining *goats from the sheep.* To do this, Jesus will decree that Satan shall be loosed.

> And when the thousand years are ended, Satan will be released from his prison and will come out to deceive the nations that are at the four corners of the earth, Gog and Magog, to gather them for battle; <u>their number is like the sand of the sea</u>. (Rev. 20:7-8)

We are not told how long Satan is loose to gather nonbelievers to fight God (which is so ridiculous yet heartbreaking). I should think it would take at least several months to a few years for Satan to ready the attack.

During this time, everyone in Christ's Kingdom (especially mortals) would be disconcerted and upset with the evil one prowling about and literally disturbing the peace Jesus had so masterfully supplied throughout the Millennium. Christ could somehow relax control to the degree necessary to allow Satan to gather the lost. For certain, Jesus would reassure and protect all resurrected saints (maybe by sequestering them in New Jerusalem).

When I pondered this, a question arose, "Might there be another Rapture event at the end of the Millennium just prior to the temporary release of Satan?" It would be consistent with what happened just before the Tribulation, and it would give safety to the earthly saints and provide them with their eternal bodies.

As prophesied, when Satan mounts the attack, Christ will dispense with him and all the millions of his deceived followers instantaneously with fire from Heaven! (cf. Rev. 20:9)

This last *assault* on God at Jerusalem will constitute the final chapter in the Progressive Revelation of God's righteousness, the total depravity of man and the incomprehensible evil of Satan.

I would expect there would be mixed emotions all around earth. There will be joy and relief that Satan has been *put away* forever. But there would also be incredible grief, as all on earth will be saddened by the number of those who had chosen to follow Satan rather than Christ. Their number would include acquaintances, friends and family members. God would undoubtedly provide great

FINAL EVENTS

comfort in this time of shock and dismay.

"Following the Millennium, Christ will turn His completely pure Kingdom over to God the Father." [1] ". . . to be merged into the eternal Kingdom, so that the ... Kingdom is perpetuated forever (1 Cor. 15:24, 28)" [2]

> After that the end will come, when he will turn the Kingdom over to God the Father, having destroyed every ruler and authority and power. For Christ must reign until he humbles all his enemies beneath his feet. And the last enemy to be destroyed is death. ... Then, when all things are under his authority, the Son will put himself under God's authority, so that God, who gave his Son authority over all things, will be utterly supreme over everything everywhere. (1Cor 15:24–26, 28   NLT)

This... "does not mean the end of our Lord's regal activity, but rather that from here onward in the unity of the Godhead He reigns with the Father as the eternal Son. There are no longer two thrones: one His Messianic throne and the other the Father's throne, as our Lord indicated in Revelation Rev. 3:21+. In the final Kingdom there is but one throne, and it is 'the throne of God and of the Lamb'" (Rev. 22:3+)[3]

THE GREAT WHITE THRONE

Before God re-creates Heaven and earth, He will judge all of mankind. Just prior to this, Jesus will again sequester all life for the time of the Great White Throne Judgment.

> Then I saw a great white throne and him who was seated on it. From his presence earth and sky fled away, and no place was found for them. And I saw the dead, great and small, standing before the throne, and books were opened.

BEYOND THE RAPTURE

Then another book was opened, which is the book of life. And the dead were judged by what was written in the books, according to what they had done. (Rev. 20:11, 12)

None of the Old Testament, New Testament or martyred Tribulation saints will be subject to this judgment (but may be privy to it). However, those Christians who were born during the Millennium (or who went into it), must be subject to this judgment or another Bema-Seat judgment by Christ (about the same time).

Once the judgment(s) is concluded, there will follow God's re-creation of the heavens and earth. All resurrected saints would remain within the eternal city, The New Jerusalem, during the re-creation. Again Jesus would cocoon all remaining life during the destruction of the old earth and heavens and then God's re-creation. Imagine the excitement and awe to be experienced by all the saints and angels as God reveals His spectacular New Heavens and Earth to them.

A *technical* question does arise: Must all millennial believers *die* to receive immortal bodies or will God exercise a Rapture-like activity to prepare them for eternity? With certainty we can say they cannot transition to the New Earth (at Millennium's end) with their sin nature. The *Rapture* possibility seems far more likely to me. Such a transformation may precede the re-creation and qualify the newly immortalized millennial humans to abide with all other resurrected saints in the New Jerusalem.

God will retain the Millennial Kingdom that Christ presents to Him, all that was good and beautiful. "There will be perpetuity of the millennial state. That is, that which characterizes the Millennial Age is not viewed as temporary but eternal." [4]

FINAL EVENTS

As marvelous as the Millennium will be, the New Heavens and Earth will surpass it. There will be no sin, no sorrow, and no death – just unending joy in righteousness. So one can think of the Millennium as a prelude to something even greater, an eternal existence with God which will surpass Christ's magnificent Millennium. Our wonderful Triune Godhead will take great pleasure in providing all their saints and angelic host a spectacular New Heavens and Earth. Please view the Epilogue for further thoughts about the New Heaven and Earth.

I conclude with two encouraging Scripture passages:

> If then you have been raised with Christ, seek the things that are above, where Christ is, seated at the right hand of God. Set your minds on things that are above, not on things that are on earth. For you have died, and your life is hidden with Christ in God. When Christ who is your life appears, then you also will appear with him in glory. (Col. 3:1–4)

> The end of the world is coming soon. Therefore, be earnest and disciplined in your prayers. Most important of all, continue to show deep love for each other, for love covers a multitude of sins. (1Pet. 4:7–8 NLT)

BEYOND THE RAPTURE

1 McClain, Alva J., *The Greatness of the Kingdom*, 31
2 Pentecost, 494
3 McClain, Alva J., *The Greatness of the Kingdom*, 513
4 Pentecost, 490

EPILOGUE

THE NEW HEAVENS AND EARTH

For look, I am ready to create new heavens and a new earth! The former ones will not be remembered; no one will think about them anymore. But be happy and rejoice forevermore over what I am about to create! For look, I am ready to create Jerusalem to be a source of joy, and her people to be a source of happiness. Jerusalem will bring me joy, and my people will bring me happiness. The sound of weeping or cries of sorrow will never be heard in her again. (Isa. 65:17-19 NET)

To try to imagine what our marvelous Creator will do in providing His saints and angels a New Earth and Heavens is presumptuous at best (Cf. Rev. 21:1-4). His creativity and capabilities know no bounds. We see His artistry, design and limitless complexity at work in our present world. He has given humans great capabilities to experience these. Our brains and five senses are needed to simply appreciate Him in the ways that we can. Think of the marvelous phenomena each human experiences through taste, touch, smell, sight and sound.

He has established exquisite beauty and given us such fulfillment and appreciation of His majestic creation. He did this by making us in His image. Taking all this into account and then compounding it with His measureless love for us, His New Heaven and Earth will leave us gasping with wonder and amazement.

All this is a mere backdrop to our being present with Him and able to know and experience Him individually and personally. So we get just a hint of what eternity with God might be like.

The topic of the New Heaven and Earth is very enigmatic due to the small amount written about it. We can however deduce certain aspects. We know it will be occupied by God, immortal humans and angels, plus all of the other mysterious godly creatures mentioned (cf. Ezk. 1:4-25 Rev. 4:6). There will however, be no mortal humans.

Everything that was wonderful in the Millennium will be present in the New Earth. All righteous humans will be preserved but will have become immortal in a manner not specified. All flora and fauna (plants and animals) will continue but probably in more wondrous form.

We can deduce this because Jesus turns His Kingdom over to God the Father and one would expect God to preserve all of its wonderful qualities and entities, *Read 1 Cor. 15:24, 28.*

God will meet all the saints' needs so that their lives will be filled with worship, fellowship, the arts, entertainment and many other activities. God will provide everything we desire (and far more) for our pleasure and amazement. God and Jesus will replace and become our Temple in resplendent glory (cf. Rev. 21:22-23)

Another phenomenon of the New Heaven and Earth is the integration of New Jerusalem into or onto the New Earth. Whereas New Jerusalem floated above earth during the Millennium, God will somehow cause this huge God-star to become part of earth. Its immense pearly gates will yawn wide in gracious welcome to all who come near. The spectacular New Jerusalem will become an ever-available

EPILOGUE: NEW HEAVENS AND EARTH

palace of God. The immortalized saints will savor every visit to God's courts and streets (read Rev. 21:10–26).

We are not told what happens to Millennial saints when they are made immortal. Does their eternal habitation become our New Jerusalem? It seems more logical that New Earth becomes their habitation and our recreation area.

The most important aspect of New Earth is that God will be such a strong part and presence to every being's life in a manner akin to the innocent and righteous era in Adam and Eve's lives. We can only vaguely imagine such a glorious and fulfilling existence. The Triune Godhead will undoubtedly reveal *themselves* in new and glorious ways.

Angelic beings will probably be integrated into our society in a special way. Previously they were God's servants on our behalf. God may allow all immortal humans friendship with those same angels who served and ministered to them invisibly.

That marvelous fellowship which typified the relationships of the resurrected in New Jerusalem will spread throughout the entire new earth. Each person will be perfect and enchanting. We won't be able to get enough of one another. Creativity, love, faith, hope and the Fruit of The Spirit will all abound. All those evils and manifestations of sinful mankind and the curse on the earth will not even be remembered (nor exist).

Because of the typical rat race most of us endure, the concept of such an existence could seem dull, even boring. But you and I know how refreshing the Lord is in so many ways. This refreshment will be all pervasive in the New Earth.

BEYOND THE RAPTURE

I have not spoken of the New Heavens but let's be imaginative. Now distant spectacles in the heavens may become a great place of exploration without need for rocket ships or space suits. God may create certain heavenly entities for us to tour that are too large or dynamic to be placed near or on earth. There could be different star clusters or exotic planets with unimaginable enchantment for us to visit.

It is logical that mortal humans will no longer be present while probably the flora and fauna will. Sinful mankind simply cannot be present in God's perfect world. However there could be 50 to 100 billion immortal humans and maybe as many angels. And yet such numbers will not be overwhelming to God, angels or immortals. Our new capabilities will allow us to easily assimilate such numbers (a staggering thought to us now).

Reproductive families as we knew it (i.e., with father, mother and children) won't exist as such. Yet, immortals from same families will be present but their relationships will be far superior to anything known before or during the Millennium. Jesus will no longer have to rule *harshly*. All beings will be so worshipful and in such harmony, that Jesus will not be forced to impose His will on anyone. As the Bible says, death will have been abolished; sin and sadness will be no more. (cf. Rev. 21:4)

God will continuously lavish His love upon each person. *Mind-boggling* is a totally inadequate phrase but a good starting point. Think of it, Our Lord and God will be *there for us* in every possible way. That utopia we all longed for will finally be ours and God will have made it superlative!

ODE TO CHRIST'S REIGN

Denny 2012

Our God among us!
His majestic presence
Amazing in power and glory

Oh the privilege
So undeserved yet
so gladly received

So many, so many
who clung to the
magnificent hope!
endeavor to absorb
His radiance, His love

Then begin the
incredible events that
initiate His reign

BEYOND THE RAPTURE

The Wedding Supper
of the Lamb is majestic
and marvelous to behold

All approving and elated
to view this display of
Christ's mercy and grace

A coronation! THE Coronation
of our King of Kings
Monarch of the universe
The most awaited event by
God, angels and humans ever

Destined to reign
from eternity past
So beloved,

ODE TO CHRIST'S REIGN

Our King of Righteousness
All hail King Jesus – monarch,
God and Savior of the world

Miracle upon miracle
Our benevolent, covenant-honoring Lord
brings the Jewish remnant to the fore
He honors them to the amazement of
every being universal

Oh Jerusalem, Jerusalem!
So long dejected and forlorn
Now the crown jewel

of the world!

Our Savior reigns

All praise to our merciful God
who keeps promises
He fashions the whole earth
as a garden of Eden
He renders so many righteous
Lord Jesus rules perfectly

One thousand years of splendor
of godliness enforced.
Perfecting His vision, His desire
His Glorious Kingdom
Hallelujah! Our God reigns!

APPENDIX
A. BIRTH PANGS

To understand the expression *birth pangs* as used in Bible prophecy, one must first familiarize himself with what Jesus Christ had to say about what is termed *endtimes*.

> Nation will go to war against nation, and kingdom against kingdom. There will be earthquakes in many parts of the world, as well as famines. But this is only the first of the birth pains with more to come. (Mark 13:8 NLT)

Jesus spoke these words as part of a response to His disciples questioning Him about His future kingdom. This is deemed the Olivet Discourse due to its being spoken on the Mount of Olives.

OLIVET DISCOURSE

The Olivet Discourse is recorded in Matthew 24:1–51, Mark 13:1–37 and Luke 17:20–37. The Scripture in Luke was written in such a way that it successfully warned and advised Christians how to survive the Roman attack (in which Jerusalem was destroyed in 70 AD). It is important to note that no Christians died in this travesty – they followed Luke's advice and fled in time; whereas, approximately one million Jews were killed. The latter number was reported by the historian, Josephus. The data about the Christians was provided by Eusebius (325 AD). "But the people of the church in Jerusalem had been commanded by a revelation, vouchsafed to approved men there before the war, to leave the city and to dwell in a certain town of Perea called Pella." (History of the Church 3:5:3)

The discourse in all three synoptic Gospels gives Christians advance notice of the events leading up to the Rapture and Tribulation. In these passages, Jesus mentions a number of signs which will alert Christians to the imminent return of Christ.

Before mentioning the signs and current happenings, let me emphasize that this is as much information as God gave and will give. The reason for the title of this appendix is:

- These are the words Jesus used to describe the signs we are to observe.

- Just as the case is with a natural birth, we can NEVER KNOW the exact time of Jesus' arrival. However, knowing the *birth pang* analogy, we can have an ever-increasing sense and expectation of His imminent return!

Think of how a normal human's birth occurs. The pregnant woman gets uncomfortably large. The baby *drops*. Then painful contractions begin and they increase in intensity and frequency. When the contractions come approximately eight minutes apart, the woman obtains the help of a doctor or midwife (because it is obvious the birth is imminent).

I believe extraordinary natural disasters will happen like the contractions of birth (with increasing intensity and frequency) prior to the Tribulation and then will crescendo into the violent havoc God wreaks upon all of earth. I am unsure of what all will comprise the *pangs* preceding the Tribulation. I suspect some of the phenomena in the following section will qualify

BIRTH PANGS

SIGNS OF THE TIMES

One very amazing phenomena is the way situations and countries are lining up so as to fulfill Bible prophecies made 2000 to 3000 years ago. The statistical probabilities for such prophecies coming to pass are astronomically implausible. Yet God has told us what is going to happen and He is causing those events to occur. Is it not incredible, that it is unfolding in our lifetime? Following is a list of the major signs of Christ's return:

1. Many false messiahs will arise.
2. Wars will increase around the world, and there will be worldwide wars.
3. There will be worldwide famine.
4. There will be earthquakes in diverse places.
5. Christians will be hated and persecuted.
6. Jews will be hated and persecuted.
7. There will be worldwide apostasy and rancor.
8. Sin will be rampant.
9. Love will become a rare commodity.
10. There will be the abomination of desolation (later during The Tribulation).
11. It will be similar to the days of Sodom and Gomorrah.
12. Peace will elude Jerusalem (and Israel) and become a major issue for the entire world (cf. Zec. 12:2–3).

PROPHECY FULFILMENT

First (and perhaps foremost) is the revival of the nation of Israel in May of 1948 (prophesied by Ezekiel [chapter

37] 2600 years ago). To the best of my knowledge, no other country has experienced such a rebirth. Once resuscitated, Israel has become God's apocalyptic timepiece. Of course Ezekiel's prophecy is only partially fulfilled at this time. The late Grant Jeffrey, in the third chapter of his book, *Armageddon*, demonstrates convincingly that the rebirth of Israel was prophesied to the exact month and year (in the Old Testament).

What is rather amazing is the cavalier attitude people can take about fulfilled prophecy. Even we Christians can so easily say, "That's neat" and move on without the miraculous registering as it should. Yet God says:

> I am God, and there is no other;
> I am God, and there is none like me.
> I make known the end from the beginning,
> from ancient times, what is still to come.
> I say, 'My purpose will stand,
> and I will do all that I please.'
> (Isa. 46:9, 10 NIV)

One prophecy thought being fulfilled is that of the fourth kingdom. "Daniel describes the final kingdom as existing of 'ten kings.' We are tempted to believe that this could not be the European Union (EU) because it has 27 members. On July 1, 2011, the EU formally invested certain critical powers always reserved to the core group known as the 'Western European Union,' in a new 'Permanent Council.' By its own choice and in its own official documents, that group is hereafter to be known as 'The Ten.'" [1]

Furthermore, the manipulations that EU is performing (in an attempt to rescue countries in dire financial straits)

BIRTH PANGS

give EU increasingly greater empire-like control.

We have seen our share of false messiahs. For example:

- Jonestown, where 918 people died at the hands of Jim Jones in Guyana in South America in November 1978.

- Waco, TX, where 82 people died following David Koresh of the Branch Davidian religious sect in April of 1993.

We have experienced two world wars and several wars involving multiple nations (for example: Korea and Vietnam). At this writing (November 2011), there are 84 wars in progress (per Answers.com) with *only* 30 wars four years previous.

As to famine, "UN warns of looming worldwide food crisis in 2013:

• Global grain reserves hit critically low levels
• Extreme weather means climate 'is no longer reliable'
• Rising food prices threaten disaster." [2]

There are severe widespread droughts in progress around the world as well. Nearly 100 million people are directly affected.

As to pestilence, I have not found anything beyond the AIDS epidemic in Africa, West Nile Virus and several deadly pandemic versions of influenza. Nowadays, a pandemic can occur at any time due to the inherent dangers of disease being spread quickly by worldwide air travel.

The prophesied *Sodom and Gomorrah* aspect of today's society is growing. The homosexual agenda is spreading worldwide.

BEYOND THE RAPTURE

Severe natural disasters also appear to be part of the mix (I regard them as potential birth pangs).

ISRAEL'S ENEMIES

The Prince of Persia (an evil angel who deterred a godly angel as he tried to reach Daniel, the prophet) appears to still be fomenting the annihilation of God's people, Israel. Iran (a significant geographic portion of ancient Persia) is bent on Israel's destruction as are most of the Middle East's Muslim countries. Iran is defiantly pursuing nuclear-weaponized missile capabilities in preparation to destroy Israel. USA, EU and NATO are only uttering passive objections (and perhaps imposing sanctions). In the meantime, Israel (under threat of annihilation) is strategizing as to when and how they must attack Iran's missile and nuclear facilities to defend themselves.

NOTE: An ancient attempt to decimate the Jewish nation was made via Haman as chronicled in the book of Esther (this too was in Persia). Satan was not only trying to eradicate the Jewish but the Messianic line as well.

The current unrest, dubbed the *Arab Spring* (summer 2011 and beyond) is occurring in approximately 12 Muslim countries and could easily lead to more Islamic theocracies (which invariably demonstrate hatred toward all Jews and become focused on Israel's eradication).

It appears that there could be a conspiracy in which The Muslim Brotherhood, Iran or some combination of Islamists are encouraging or facilitating the toppling of dictators who enforce secular regimes. Once the dictator is ousted, then either under the guise of a democratic process

BIRTH PANGS

(or directly), an Islamic government is *voted in*. The next step is to invoke Sharia law. Morocco and Tunisia are going down this path. Egypt suffered through six months of the Brotherhood's rule and overthrew it. More *secular dictatorships* are being threatened.

Another situation which recently unfolded is that USA has prematurely left Iraq and Afghanistan. Experts in the Middle East predicted that Iran will quickly annex Iraq. As of July 2014, Iraq stands tattered amidst sectarian warfare and so does Afghanistan.

An exciting note is that <u>hundreds of thousands of Muslims are turning to Christ</u>.

On the Jewish religious front, various groups in Israel are taking measures to reestablish temple worship. One group has prepared all the furnishings needed for temple worship and is training potential priests as to how to conduct services. The Temple Institute located in Jerusalem trains rabbis to be priests in the yet to be rebuilt Temple. Training includes the ancient Jewish sacrificial rites. This institute also is studying the trappings of temple worship. They have been re-creating vessels appropriate for Temple worship. Their institute can be accessed at templeinstitute.org.

During the same time frame, Jewish Archeologist Asher Kaufman has conducted archaeological studies and believes that the Herodian temple was 100 meters northwest of the Dome of the Rock. If this information is validated and acted upon, a temple could be built there. You can read more about this at:

http:// tribulationsaints.com/newjewishtemple.html

BEYOND THE RAPTURE

ISRAEL'S CURRENT DILEMMA

Israel's prophesied enemy nations have already aligned themselves against her and are taking increasingly threatening and substantive actions. The very fact that these countries are harassing and menacing Israel is a fulfillment of prophecy in itself. Israel has been subject to attacks since it was first *reborn* in May of 1948.

There are approximately 26 countries (prophesied in Ezekiel 38 and elsewhere in the Bible) that will first come against Israel during the Tribulation. Most of these countries have already arrayed themselves against Israel. Turkey is growing estranged from Israel. Turkey is one of the enemies in Ezekiel's prophecy. Two larger, non-Muslim countries prophesied to come against Israel are Russia (Gog and Magog) and China (kings of the East). Both have aligned themselves with several Muslim countries and against Israel. In past Israeli conflicts, Russia supplied weaponry, military training and logistics to Israel's enemies

Using simple statistics, I have calculated the odds of just 6 of those countries fulfilling the prophecies in Ezekiel 38. The chances are one in 52.48 trillion (and this is not taking into account its happening 2600 years later – statistically speaking).

The Middle-East situation is so volatile and dynamic that it would be near impossible to write a book about it. It would be more realistic to try to blog events (and that would keep more than one person very busy).

I cannot imagine the pervading fear and stress of Israel's people, as they experience the on-going harassment coming from the surrounding nations aligned against them. I can only begin to relate with the feelings they are having by recalling the constant tension and worry we American citizens experienced during the cold war (with the continuous threat of nuclear attack from Russia). This phenomenon was most palpable during the Cuban Missile Crisis.

In addition to this, anti-Semitism is on the rise in Europe. A significant portion of the European Union favors the Palestinians over Israel. In 2011, one of the top three political parties in Hungary became openly anti-Semitic. You can note in the 2008 Pew chart following, that Hungary did not even rate mention at that time.

Europe seems to have forgotten the inherent dangers of Islam and has, by and large, embraced Muslim immigration. In addition, some have allowed it to create an atmosphere dangerous to the Jewish people. Therefore there has been an exodus of Jews from certain countries – Norway, Denmark, Belgium, France and Hungary. Web sites such as jewishvirtuallibrary.org and danielpipes.org are tracking such incidents. There are over a million Jews in Europe.

"Abbas (The leader of the Palestine Authority [PA]) submitted a formal request for recognition as an independent nation to the United Nations Security Council (in the fall of 2011). The Security Council did not accede to their wishes; however, UNESCO has recognized them as a nation. The PA could also ask the General Assembly to extend recognition."[3] Whatever happens, Abbas has already advanced PA's cause.

In the last few years, Islam has expanded from being

BEYOND THE RAPTURE

1/6th of the world's population to 1/5th. The Muslim population has been increasing proportionately within Israel itself.

ANTI-SEMITISM

Following is a re-creation of a Pew Research Center chart of the rise of anti-Semitism in Europe from a poll taken in 2008: It is based on anti-Semitism incidents per year.

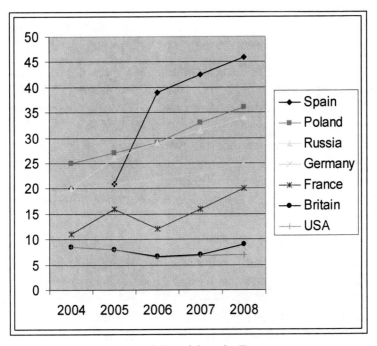

Anti-Semitism in Europe

The following chart shows worldwide anti-Semitic incidents 2000-2012:

BIRTH PANGS

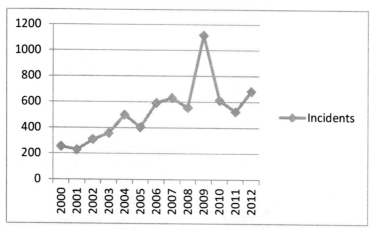

Worldwide Violent Anti-Semitic Incidents
(from the EMET Blog 20JUL14)

The following is an article from the Haaretz News Media, Tel Aviv:

"Study: Anti-Semitism in Europe hit new high in 2009 (Published 11.04.10) Tel Aviv University study: By Canaan Liphshiz.

The worldwide increase in anti-Semitic attacks following Israel's 2009 incursion into Gaza hit the U.K. and France the hardest compared to all other European countries, according to Tel Aviv University's watchdog on anti-Semitism.

The total number of anti-Semitic incidents – as they are defined by the institute – was a record number of 1,129 in 2009, compared to 559 in 2008. The institute recorded 566 incidents of vandalism targeting Jewish property worldwide in 2009, constituting 49 percent of all incidents." [4]

BEYOND THE RAPTURE

During July and August of 2014, Israel again defended itself against the terrorist group, Hamas. They assailed Israel with over 2000 rockets (from Gaza). Israel was forced to go into Gaza Strip to dismantle the Hamas rocketry infrastructure. The treacherous and cowardly Hamas launch rockets from civilian areas - schools, mosques and public institutions to assure that any Israeli reprisals will kill civilians and draw the condemnation of the world. As usual, too much of the world turned a blind eye to Hamas' terrorism and focused on Palestinian deaths resulting from Israel's actions. Anti-Semitism activities again spiked worldwide.

One of the most shocking developments of anti-Semitism in recent years is that coming from a sector of the Christian church. A rising number of those embracing Replacement 'theology' are expressing increasingly hateful attitudes towards Israel.

EARTHQUAKES

Another apparent sign is the significant increase in earthquakes. I have found the following statistics on the web. These statistics show that magnitude 7+ earthquakes have increased 17 fold, from 12 in 1863 to 208 by the end of 2013. (190 were projected through 2014).

EARTHQUAKE DATA

DATES	PERIOD	#. EARTHQUAKES (Magnitude. > 6.99)
1863 to 1900 incl	38 yrs	12
1901 to 1938 incl	38 yrs	53
1939 to 1976 incl	38 yrs	71
1977 to <u>2014</u> incl *	38 yrs	208 *(through 2013)

BIRTH PANGS

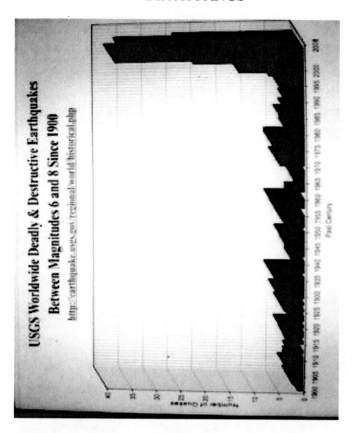

NOTE: Though blurry, the overall chart is important. The reason is that the Earthquake Data Chart showed earthquakes magnitude > 6.99. The last chart shows those between magnitude 6 and 8.

Currently significant earthquakes data can be found at: http://earthquake.usgs.gov/earthquakes/eqinthenews/

BEYOND THE RAPTURE

1 Lindsey, Hal (Excerpted from The Hal Report, 5AUG11)
2. The Observer, October 13, 2012
3. Lindsey, January 21, 2012
4. Haaretz.com (Excerpted from Study: Anti-Semitism in Europe hit new high in 2009)

APPENDIX
B. PROGRESSIVE REVELATION

INTRODUCTION

Some theologians have posited that the biblical record and natural history constitute evidence presented in a courtroom scene in Heaven (that is, a phenomenon by which God is demonstrating to all heavenly beings His overall righteousness and wisdom).

> God's purpose in all this was to use the church to display His wisdom in its rich variety to all the unseen rulers and authorities in the heavenly places. (Eph. 3:10 NLT)

We get another hint of *courtroom* action in this cryptic verse;

> Now have come the salvation and the power and the kingdom of our God, and the authority of his Christ. For the accuser of our brothers, who accuses them before our God day and night, has been hurled down. (Rev. 12:10. NLT)

Another equally cryptic passage is found in Job 1:6–12 (in which God challenges Satan regarding Job). We cannot begin to fathom the reasons or scope of this drama in Heaven. This will be but one of God's many revelations to us once we are present with Him.

Another dimension provided the heavenly host is the way God unfolds His overall plan and strategy for handling the sin of both angels and humans.

Down through the ages, God has provided different scenarios in which humans could have a relationship with Him. With Adam and Eve, He had direct relationship with a pure and sinless couple.

After they *fell*, God repeatedly changed the paradigm regarding His relationship to mankind. In so doing, He has shown that man's sinful nature continually causes him to reject an all loving, merciful God (individually and collectively). Mankind has done this regardless of how wonderful God has shown Himself to be.

Israel is the classic and yet pathetic example of this. Just the events from their deliverance from Egypt to their being condemned to wander in the wilderness shows what a faithless and reprobate nation they were.

Yet in God's overall plan, grace and mercy, He intends to restore Israel to a place of incredible privilege, keeping His promises and covenants. This is a large scale example of how he treats any and all who seek Him. He demonstrates His grace (giving us wonderful things we do not deserve) and mercy (not giving us the exile and eternal punishment we do deserve).

So with the Millennium and the godly eternity to follow, God concludes His plan of the ages.

> In all wisdom and insight making known to us the mystery of his will, according to his purpose, which he set forth in Christ as a plan for the fullness of time, to unite all things in him, things in Heaven and things on earth. (Eph. 1:8b–10)

God makes known to all the heavenly host the mystery of His will in the courtroom of Heaven. The vindication of all He has done will be complete, perfect and beyond reproach.

PROGRESSIVE REVELATION

DISPENSATIONS

In Dispensational Theology, it is common practice to divide the spiritual history of the world into seven (7) dispensations (some say four, some add more). "Each dispensation is said to represent a different way in which God deals with man. Some writers also believe that each involves a different testing of Man. "'these periods are marked off in Scripture by some change in God's method of dealing with mankind, in respect to two questions: of sin, and of man's responsibility,' explained C. I. Scofield " [1]

Beginning with the first dispensation (known as *Innocence – Adam and Eve*), each dispensation starts with a new expectation from God for mankind and ends after a catastrophic failure. Each era demonstrates (to God's heavenly host and eventually to mankind) that the grace of God is ignored and mankind as a whole fails to achieve anything approaching godliness. This last statement is tempered by the presence of the Holy Spirit on earth and His being active within the lives of Christians during the Church Age.

BEYOND THE RAPTURE

DISPENSATIONS CHART

DISPENSATION	GOD'S EXPECTATION	FAILURE/ PENALTY
1. Innocence (Adam to the Fall)	1. Obedience/ Relationship	1. Ate Forbidden Fruit **Spiritual death/ Curse**
2. Conscience (Fall to Noah)	2. Obey conscience	2. All of society Became wicked **Flood**
3. Government (Noah to Abraham)	3. Godly governments	3. Tower of Babel **Scatter/confused Languages**
4. Patriarchal Rule (Abraham to Moses)	4. Godly patriarchs	4. Israel did not enter the land **Wandered Desert 40 years**
5. Mosaic Law (Moses to Christ)	5. Israel keep God's law	5. Rejection of Messiah **Jews "blind"/ set aside**
6. Grace (Church age) Christ until the Rapture	6. People saved in every tongue, tribe and nation	6. Apostasy worldwide **Tribulation judgments**
7. Reign of Christ (1000 years)	7. Accomplish all of His purposes	7. Satan-led rebellion **Great White Throne**

1. C. I. Scofield (Wikipedia) web

APPENDIX
C. MARY'S FAMILY

JESUS' BIRTH

Mary will be celebrated for her faith and endurance throughout Jesus' 33 years here. She endured the ridicule of gossips and the songs of drunkards in taverns for her perceived fornication due to her pregnancy before wedlock (cf. Psa. 69:8, 12, John 8:41). She endured even the breach between her children and Jesus as they became uncertain as to who he really was.

Other things which we tend to overlook are satanic attacks. Perhaps Satan attempted to cause Mary to spontaneously abort with the long and dangerous trip to Bethlehem. She had to give birth with only Joseph helping and no midwife and perhaps no experience (on her part) with a newborn.

Prior to Jesus' birth, Mary also experienced the loss of not having the traditional marriage ceremony (and its normal celebration and jubilation with relatives and friends).

One of the thoughts which probably sustained her through all of the hardships she bore would have been her incredible encounter with the angel Gabriel. He said:

> You have found favor with God! You will conceive and give birth to a son, and you will name him Jesus. <u>He will be very great and will be called the Son of the Most High. The Lord God will give him the throne of his ancestor David</u>. (Luke 1:30b–32)

BEYOND THE RAPTURE

Also recall Mary's Magnificat – how she praised God during her visit to her cousin Elizabeth:

> Oh, how my soul praises the Lord. How my spirit rejoices in God my Savior! For he took notice of his lowly servant girl, and from now on all generations will call me blessed. For the Mighty One is holy, and he has done great things for me. (Luke 1:46b–49 NLT)

THE FLIGHT TO EGYPT

The arrival of the Magi would have helped to strengthen her faith and probably more significantly, that of Joseph. Then within months or a few years, they experienced a complete upheaval in their lives, having to flee to Egypt – a nation with a different language, culture and religion. God would have had to go before them so that Joseph could find work and a place to stay. They were forced to exist as isolated aliens, unable to visit a synagogue or make the annual trek to Jerusalem.

Undoubtedly they were lonely, missing their friends, siblings and relatives. Without the trappings of Judaism, they would have struggled to continue their way of life, find appropriate food and withstand the treatment of the Egyptians. The Egyptians would have been practicing their strange religion all around them and probably questioned why they did not participate. At every turn, Satan would have tried to give them grief – the need for supernatural intervention would have been ongoing.

When they returned to Nazareth, Joseph might have had to start over (they had remained in Bethlehem until the escape to Egypt). Who knows how well (or long) the gifts of the Magi sustained them. Mary and Joseph may have returned with another newborn. Whatever the case, Mary

MARY'S FAMILY

bore four more sons (cf. Mark 6:3) and at least two daughters.

LIFE IN NAZARETH

So their lives were hard. They had none of the modern conveniences that we have. So the washing of clothes, diapers and dishes was all done in a crude way. The same was true of food preparation and cooking. Firewood had to be gathered for all cooking as well as providing heat in winter.

Joseph was a carpenter and probably toiled from sunup to sundown to gather materials for his trade, take customer orders, fashion or repair household items as well as wagons, carriages and more. In other words, he had little time to assist Mary.

Emotionally, Mary had to be very strong and courageous – bearing the ongoing taunts and disapproval, and trying to help her children handle the cruelty of other kids. She sheltered her children from her pain and struggled to fully understand Jesus.

But despite all this, Mary remained strong in her faith. It was she who called for Jesus' first miracle (John 2:1-12). It was she who endeavored to mediate between Jesus and His brothers (John 7:5). As Simeon predicted (cf. Luke 2:34–35), it was she who suffered most of all as Jesus was condemned, crucified and buried. Jesus knew all this, so (undoubtedly) He mentored John such that he would take good care of Mary when He departed.

BEYOND THE RAPTURE

JESUS' MINISTRY

Mary was the first of her family to believe in His Messiahship, the first to become Christian. She probably was an influential Christian in the lives of other women and their children in terms of her faith.

Even after her death, Satan continued his assault on her by furthering the mother-child worship begun with Nimrod's wife and child. He plugged her into a *holy family,* that is, God the Father, Mary the Mother and Jesus the son. This is embodied in Mary worship. The deception of Roman Catholicism persists 2000 years later. I am sure Jesus has protected her from this (in Heaven).

Growing up, Jesus siblings would have experienced Him as a totally godly, loving and caring older brother. "Jesus grew in stature, wisdom and in the favor of God and people." (Luke 2:52) But with their sin nature, it would have been frustrating to attempt to compete with Him in any way.

When Jesus began His ministry and left them to fend for themselves, the family was undoubtedly torn. Jesus had become the family leader and was uncle to His siblings' children.

Despite what their mother had shared with them, it was difficult for Jesus' siblings to fathom His being their Messiah. They had suffered from Nazareth's rejection of Him and could not grasp their brother being God. He was so gentle and meek, never revealing who He was or would become.

MARY'S FAMILY

THE CRUCIFIXION

As Jesus' ministry was completed, He was brutally executed. Again they would be torn by doubt and ridicule from their town's lowlife ("Could any good come from Nazareth?" – per Nathanael, the disciple, [cf. John 1:46]). The whole town of Nazareth rejected Jesus' claims and tried to murder Him (Luke 4:29). So they had much to overcome. Not until His resurrection appearances were His brothers (at least two, James and Judas [Jude] who wrote two NT books) persuaded of His being Messiah.

Mary was probably influential in winning James and Jude to Christ. She will be a hero of the faith and hold a place of honor throughout the Millennium and all eternity. To what degree will this be true of Joseph – we know so very little of him?

JOSEPH

Joseph is an OT saint; Mary a NT saint. He would (and will) be known as a protector, provider and mentor for Jesus; they undoubtedly had a very close relationship. Both Jesus and especially Mary would have grieved at his death. We do not know why Jesus did not raise him from the dead or why Joseph is *out of the picture.*

Recalling how Jesus wept before raising Lazarus, I would venture that He would have wept at the death of Joseph (especially because He *could not* raise him from the dead or heal him from what killed him). His is a history most will be excited to hear. Joseph himself may tell us all about it.

BEYOND THE RAPTURE

Joseph could easily have lived until the time immediately before Jesus began His ministry. We hear nothing about Jesus between the ages of twelve and thirty. Therefore it is not presumptuous to believe Joseph lived until close to the time of Christ's ministry. Joseph could have been as old as 30 when he married Mary, so he could have reached age 60. Life expectancy was shorter in those days. Whatever the case, the details of Joseph's death will remain a puzzler.

APPENDIX
D. SPIRITUAL BEINGS

ANGELS

Following are some observations from the Bible about spiritual beings. Jesus Himself exhibited some of these traits in His post-resurrection body and in His pre-incarnate appearances.

Angels are usually undetectable by any human senses. However, they seem to be able to morph into visible, human form. Examples of this are the angel Gabriel's appearance to Jesus' mother, Mary and Zacharias, father of John the Baptist. They can speak and understand human language(s). They probably have their own heavenly language as well.

Following is the Prophet Daniel's description of an angel which appeared in his vision:

> I lifted up my eyes and looked, and behold, a man clothed in linen, with a belt of fine gold from Uphaz around his waist. His body was like beryl, his face like the appearance of lightning, his eyes like flaming torches, his arms and legs like the gleam of burnished bronze, and the sound of his words like the sound of a multitude. (Dan. 10:5–6)

Apparently they are able to change size (even astronomically); for example,: the angel standing with one foot on the ocean and one on earth; and another angel pouring something on the sun to darken it. These appearances are quite a contrast from angels appearing as humans. (cf. Rev. 10:1–2, 16:8)

When they morph into detectable form, they can be

experienced tactilely as well as visually, for example, the angel who struck Peter (Acts 12:7). Another example is when the angels took Lot, his wife and daughters by the hand and led them out of Sodom and Gomorrah (Gen. 19:16).

They seem to have our 5 senses (touch, smell, taste, sight, and hearing) and understandably more (considering that they exist in domains beyond humans [cf. all of Genesis 18]).

They probably experience at least ten dimensions (the dimensions conjectured by ancient Hebrew scholars and certain scientists today). This is not difficult to accept as one ponders their imperceptible ministry to us humans (who experience four dimensions – height, width, depth and time).

They can cause a variety of effects to earthly entities as varied as the weather (cf. Job 1:16, 19) and locks and gates (cf. Acts 12:7–10). Also, Gabriel struck Zacharias dumb until after the birth of his son, John the Baptist (Luke 1:20).

Spiritual beings demonstrate they are not impacted or impeded by the lack of atmosphere, extreme variations in temperature, air pressure, or gravity,

We will be like angels in some ways:

For in the resurrection they neither marry nor are given in marriage, but are like angels in Heaven. (Mat. 22:30)

The quality of angels that fascinates humankind the most is their ever-present yet unseen nature. I realized an analogy that illustrates this phenomenon. Whenever we are afloat on a body of water, we might see an occasional water

SPIRITUAL BEINGS

creature. But most activity though close to us, normally remains undetectable. The angelic realm exists around us in like manner. The following Bible story illustrates this phenomenon wonderfully:

> One night the king of Aram sent a great army with many chariots and horses to surround the city.
>
> When the servant of the man of God got up early the next morning and went outside, there were troops, horses, and chariots everywhere. "Oh, sir, what will we do now?" the young man cried to Elisha.
>
> "Don't be afraid!" Elisha told him. "For there are more on our side than on theirs!" Then Elisha prayed, "O LORD, open his eyes and let him see!" The LORD opened the young man's eyes, and when he looked up, <u>he saw that the hillside around Elisha was filled with horses and chariots of fire</u>.
> (2 Kin. 6:14 –17 NLT)

NOTE: These thoughts about angels are far from exhaustive. To gain a better overall perspective, one could read a comprehensive book such as *Angels*, by C. Fred Dickason.

<u>JESUS</u>

Jesus displayed His spiritual personage in several ways. He made numerous pre-incarnate appearances in which He was called *the Angel of the Lord*. In some such instances, He is only mentioned as speaking to people. When he appeared to Gideon and to Abraham, He appeared as human. However, in His appearance to Manoah and his wife, He demonstrated the His supernatural qualities:

> And when the flame went up toward Heaven from the altar, the Angel of the LORD went up in the flame of the altar. Now Manoah and his wife were watching, and they fell on their

faces to the ground. (Jud. 13:20)

During His first advent, He was "born in the likeness of men" and "found in human form" (cf. Php. 2:7c¬8a). However, He exhibited supernatural qualities in many instances. He passed through crowd intent on stoning Him in Nazareth unhindered. He walked on water. He appeared in His glory on the Mount of Transfiguration.

In His post-resurrection appearances, His disciples (the larger circle of them) struggled to recognize Him (for example, those on the road to Emmaus and Mary at the tomb [cf. Luke 24:31). Also, He appeared to the Apostles in a closed room without the need for an open door or window. Then in His ascension, He rose through the air into the clouds and continued all the way to Heaven.

Yet, when Jesus appeared to His disciples (several times), He encouraged them to touch and observe Him.

> And he said to them, "Why are you troubled, and why do doubts arise in your hearts? See my hands and my feet, that it is I myself. Touch me, and see. For a spirit does not have flesh and bones as you see that I have." And when he had said this, he showed them his hands and his feet. And while they still disbelieved for joy and were marveling, he said to them, "Have you anything here to eat?" They gave him a piece of broiled fish, and he took it and ate before them. (Luke. 24:38–43)

Do take note that Jesus displayed a normal human appearance. He displayed the standard configuration of head, torso, arms, legs, feet and hands.

In the first chapter of Revelation, John sees Jesus in the magnificent scene with the seven churches. In another instance, Jesus appears as a Lamb slain. In yet another, He descends to earth on a white horse. Whether such

SPIRITUAL BEINGS

appearances remain symbolic within the pages of Scripture or Jesus is actually changing form and size, we will not know until we *get there.*

Grudem, in his *Bible Doctrine* book, makes mention of Jesus' body having spatial limitations (pg. 266). Perhaps this is true; however, Jesus is a member of our Triune Godhead. Therefore, He is omnipresent. I conclude that although Jesus has an eternal physical body, He can (and does) transcend His body in ways we may never understand.

> For in Christ lives all the fullness of God in a human body. (Col. 2:9 NLT)

Here is another thought about Christ's eternal body. Isaiah, the prince of prophets, says this regarding Christ's first advent:

> For he grew up before him like a young plant, and like a root out of dry ground; he had no form or majesty that we should look at him, and no beauty that we should desire him. (Isa. 53:2)

I would suggest Jesus' post-resurrection body (and especially His face) is majestic and has great beauty. When Jesus was on the Mount of Transfiguration, Scripture says that as He began to pray, "His face was transformed ... " (cf. Luke 9:29 NLT)

THE HUMAN SOUL (SPIRIT)

We have some hints as to what happens to our human soul (spirit) at death. Jesus' story of Lazarus and the rich man gives us clues (cf. Luke 16:19–31).

> Finally, the poor man died and was carried by the angels to be with Abraham. The rich man also died and was buried,

and his soul went to the place of the dead. There, in torment, he saw Abraham in the far distance with Lazarus at his side. (Luke 16:22–23 NLT)

Let us examine this passage to determine what qualities of the soul we can observe:

- Our soul (and/or spirit) has a bodily quality – "was carried by the angels."
- Our souls have locality – "to be with Abraham."
- OT souls immediately went to be in Abraham's Bosom or Torments

The next passage depicts a dialog between a deceased rich man and Abraham:

The rich man shouted, 'Father Abraham, have some pity! Send Lazarus over here to dip the tip of his finger in water and cool my tongue. I am in anguish in these flames.' (Luke 16:24 NLT)

But Abraham said to him, "Son, remember that during your lifetime you had everything you wanted, and Lazarus had nothing. So now he is here being comforted, and you are in anguish. And besides, there is a great chasm separating us. No one can cross over to you from here, and no one can cross over to us from there." (Luke 16:25 NLT)

What can we observe from these verses?

- Our souls can experience comfort or pain
- Our souls can speak
- Our souls can see and hear
- Our souls can reason
- Our souls are affected by boundaries

Then the rich man said, "Please, Father Abraham, at least send him to my father's home. For I have five brothers, and I want him to warn them so they don't end up in this place of

SPIRITUAL BEINGS

torment."

But Abraham said, "Moses and the prophets have warned them. Your brothers can read what they wrote."

The rich man replied, "No, Father Abraham! But if someone is sent to them from the dead, then they will repent of their sins and turn to God."

But Abraham said, "If they won't listen to Moses and the prophets, they won't listen even if someone rises from the dead." (Luke 16:27 – 31   NLT)

Last observations

- Our souls have memory of our mortal life.
- Our souls can have compassion (and probably other human emotions)
- Condemned souls can experience rebuke
- Condemned souls can plead and receive answers

Because Jesus told this story about an OT situation, it is important to note that NT saints' destination at death is quite different:

We are confident, I say, and willing rather to be absent from the body, and to be present with the Lord. (2 Cor. 5:8   KJV)

In other words, nowadays when Christians expire, all that they are (minus their human bodies and sin nature), is immediately translated into the presence of Christ. There they await the rapture and their new immortal bodies.

Some prominent Christian scholars believe that when Christians die, they receive an intermediate body. They come to this conclusion from exegeting Revelation 6:9-11. In particular, they find the words about souls receiving white robes indicative of their having bodies.

When he opened the fifth seal, I saw under the altar the

souls of those who had been slain because of the word of God and the testimony they had maintained. They called out in a loud voice, "How long, Sovereign Lord, holy and true, until you judge the inhabitants of the earth and avenge our blood?" <u>Then each of them was given a white robe,</u> and they were told to wait a little longer, until the full number of their fellow servants, their brothers and sisters, were killed just as they had been. (Rev. 6:9-11 NIV)

NOTE: This exploration of the human soul is primarily meant to show the state and capabilities of departed Christians' souls until the Rapture.

APPENDIX
E. ANCIENT JEWISH WEDDING PRACTICES

And their parallel to Christ and the Church

MARRIAGE COVENANT AND BRIDE PRICE

When a man wanted to marry a woman in ancient Israel, he would bring a contract (or covenant) he had crafted to present to her and her father at her home. The contract was his offer for her hand. Most important was the bride price, that is, what he would pay to marry her. This was to be paid to her father. This price was usually considerable. Daughters were considered less valuable than sons; therefore, the bride price compensated the father for his expense to raise her. More importantly, it indicated her suitor's love for her.

THE CUP

As part of the ceremony (once the father had agreed), the suitor would offer a glass of wine to his intended. If she drank the wine, it would indicate her agreement. The glass of wine sealed their betrothal and was as legally binding as marriage. A typical betrothal period lasted one to two years. During this time both the bride and bridegroom prepared for the marriage, yet without seeing one another.

BEYOND THE RAPTURE

GIFTS FOR THE BRIDE

During betrothal, the bridegroom would send the bride special gifts. These gifts reinforced his love and hopefully helped her remember him during the long wait.

MIKVEH

As part of the engagement, the bride would partake of a Mikveh, or cleansing bath. To this day, in Orthodox Judaism, a bride cannot marry without a Mikveh.

PREPARING A PLACE

During the betrothal time, the bridegroom prepared their wedding chamber. This was typically built inside his father's house. It had to be a place of beauty. The bride and groom would spend their first seven days there. This chamber had to be built to his father's specifications, and the wedding could only begin once his father approved. If the bridegroom were asked about the wedding date, he might respond, "It is not for me to know; only my father knows."

WAITING BRIDE CONSECRATED

While the bridegroom was away making preparations, the bride was considered consecrated or *bought with a price*. If she went out, she would wear a veil so others would know she was betrothed. During this time she prepared herself for the marriage. During her entire life, she had planned and saved for her wedding. She now prepared further by beautifying herself for the bridegroom. The time

ANCIENT JEWISH WEDDING PRACTICES

of her wedding (when her groom would come for her) was a mystery, so she always had to be ready. Since a bridegroom typically came for his bride in the middle of the night, she would have to have her lamp and her belongings ready at all times. Her bridesmaids (often some were her sisters) would also be waiting, keeping their lamps trimmed in anticipation of the late night festivities.

BRIDEGROOM FETCHES HIS BRIDE

When the wedding chamber was deemed ready, the father would inform the bridegroom. He would then go *abduct* his bride secretly, like a thief at night and take her to his wedding chamber. As the bridegroom approached the bride's home, he would shout and blow the shofar (ram's horn) to warn her to gather her belongings.

7 DAYS IN THE WEDDING CHAMBER

The wedding couple honeymooned seven days in the wedding chamber. Their friends would wait nearby. The guests celebrated until the bride and bridegroom emerged from the chamber.

MARRIAGE SUPPER

Once they emerged, the newly-weds would participate in a feast with friends and family. There would be joyous celebrating during this feast with some form of grand finale.

DEPART FOR HOME

Once the festivities had concluded, the bride and groom

would depart to their home which he had prepared.

PARALLELS TO CHRIST AND THE CHURCH

I have intentionally waited to draw these parallels between Christ and The Church until now, to allow you to have some *aha* moments (in case you were not fully familiar with these traditions until now).

Jesus came to the home of His bride (earth) to present His marriage contract. His covenant (with His Bride – the church) was the New Covenant. The bride price was stated in the upper room with the first *communion*. Remember Jesus' words, "This bread is my body broken for you." (cf. Luke 22:19) The cup of wine was served by Jesus to His disciples and they symbolically partook for all who would ever become Christians (Jesus' bride). He stated His new covenant as they were about to partake:

> And likewise the cup after they had eaten, saying, "This cup that is poured out for you is the new covenant in my blood." (Luke 22:20)

The Bride Price was His crucifixion. Jesus offered this for Israel (and also for the entire world).

The Gifts for the Bride are the Holy Spirit and His ministry and spiritual gifts. The gifts are the supernatural abilities which Christians need to fulfill the needs of the church. These gifts are described in Romans 12, 1Corinthians 12, Ephesians 4 and 1 Peter 4.

Our Mikveh is twofold. We receive the gift of eternal life from the Holy Spirit and we have all been baptized into one body by one Spirit (the word Mikveh means baptism). Secondly, we obey and acknowledge God by being

ANCIENT JEWISH WEDDING PRACTICES

baptized as a testimony to our belief in Him.

In him you also, when you heard the word of truth, the gospel of your salvation, and believed in him, were sealed with the promised Holy Spirit, who is the guarantee of our inheritance until we acquire possession of it, to the praise of his glory. (Eph.1:13–14)

Jesus told His disciples that He was going to *prepare a place* for them.

Where the seven-day *honeymoon* occurs or what will take place are things we do not know. As Jesus stated, "It is not for me to know; only my Father knows." (Mat. 24:36) But we do know that this honeymoon is going to give us ecstasy beyond measure.

Jesus' waiting bride, the church, is consecrated (individually) by the sanctifying work of the Holy Spirit.

Jesus comes for His bride at the Rapture, that marvelous, ultimate event we each long to experience.

There is general agreement that the wedding chamber ceremony and *honeymoon* will occur during the seven years of the Tribulation *(Ironic, is it not?).*

Due to the various events which must precede the Marriage Supper, it will most logically occur in the first days of the Millennium. It is an eternally important event referred to as the Wedding Supper of the Lamb.

A significant number of Bible scholars believe that the New Jerusalem will be our eternal home.

Overall, this marvelous marriage analogy portrays events leading to Christ's Millennium in such a definitive manner that it virtually dictates the order of events (coming together like the pieces of a puzzle).

BEYOND THE RAPTURE

The original document and majority of this appendix was written by Burke and Glenna Magee.[1]

---

1 Magee, Burke and Glenna, *Weddings of Ancient Israel, A Picture of the Messiah,* web

APPENDIX
F. MY "PROPHECY" TESTIMONY

I had been seeking serious answers for some time. My life had turned into one of desperation. In February of 1970, I confessed to God that I had been seeing with my physical eyes my whole life and that I had really made a mess of things. I asked Him to open my spiritual eyes. By God's grace, my heart was right and God came into my life, opened my *eyes* and granted me new life in Jesus.

In those first months, an amazing phenomenon took place. The Holy Spirit began teaching me through a variety of sources (although I did not know who He was at the time). He taught me from what I remembered of the Bible – causing me to understand many things for the first time. He used every medium I chose, whether the Bible (I had started reading the New Testament), the radio, TV or different venues at church. It was a very precious time, one which I will never forget. One of Jesus' sayings was particularly poignant to me at that time:

> I came that they may have life and have it abundantly. (John 10:10b)

I remember two of many very important *finds*. I really did not understand who Jesus was (even though I had accepted Him as savior). Not until I read the passage in which Jesus declared, "Before Abraham was, I Am." (cf. John 8:58) did I understand Him to be God. The other *find* occurred as I participated in Evangelism Explosion training. During that time, I discovered the concepts of Heaven – something I had not even considered.

A few years later I read the *hot* Christian book on the

market, *The Late Great Planet Earth* (by Hal Lindsey). As a result, I became acquainted with end-times prophecy and parts of the Old Testament.

One of the most important things in recent history occurred when I was a young teen. Israel was reborn as a nation in 1948 (as had been prophesied thousands of years prior by Ezekiel). I was unaware of this at the time and no one among my family or acquaintances took special note either. And the funniest thing happened. The barbershop quartets in our area (of which my dad and I took part) had great fun singing a song entitled, *Dry Bones!* Yet not one mention was made of what the song meant (that is, its recounting the prophecy of Ezekiel 37). No one praised God for the miraculous nature of the Israel's rebirth.

Back to the present; I feel fortunate that we are living in such exciting days. As they say, *the plot thickens.* Somehow, I have not been totally seduced (by our myopic news media) into ignoring most things which occur outside of USA. I currently rely heavily on the following sites for what is going on around the globe and in particular, the Middle East and the European Union:

- Listening to the weekly podcasts from the website, ProphecyToday.com
- Reading daily posts from *The Times of Israel* and WorthyNews.com
- Reading periodic Hal Lindsey reports
- Reading the news section of both HalLindsey.com and RaptureReady.com

I think the following verses have great importance to every Christian, today!

MY PROPHECY TESTIMONY

> But you are not in darkness, brothers, for that day to surprise you like a thief. For you are all children of light, children of the day. We are not of the night or of the darkness. So then let us not sleep, as others do, but let us keep awake and be sober. (1 The. 5:4-6)

This ends my testimony in one sense, but I feel compelled to convey a very important message to everyone who reads this book. Its content is the heart of my testimony. The next section is directed to those who have not established a personal relationship with God through Jesus Christ. It contains instructions about how to transition into this relationship with God and receive His gift of eternal life.

THE GOSPEL

> Examine yourselves, to see whether you are in the faith. Test yourselves that Jesus Christ is in you? – unless indeed you fail to meet the test! (2 Cor. 13:10)

The Gospel message that I hope you know, understand and accept is as follows:

- Confess that there is nothing you have done (or can do) that will <u>earn</u> you an eternal relationship with God or a place in Heaven!

  > For by grace you have been saved through faith. And this is not your own doing; it is the gift of God, not a result of works, so that no one may boast. (Eph. 2:8–9)

- <u>Confess</u> that you have sinned against God and others during your lifetime.

  > For all have sinned and fall short of the glory of God. (Rom. 3:23)

- Realize that <u>eternal life</u> (and a rich relationship with

BEYOND THE RAPTURE

God) <u>is a gift</u> which can only be received through belief in Jesus the Messiah.

> For the wages of sin is death, but the free gift of God is eternal life in Christ Jesus our Lord. (Ro. 6:23)

- <u>Accept</u> that Jesus Christ (being The Son of God and God the Son) came to earth, lived a perfect life and then went to the cross to pay for our sins. That He arose from the grave, resides at the right hand of God and offers eternal life to whosoever believes in Him.

> For God so loved the world, that he gave his only Son, that whoever believes in him should not perish but have eternal life. (John 3:16)

- <u>Take action</u> as prescribed in the following verses.

> If you confess with your mouth that Jesus is Lord and believe in your heart that God raised him from the dead, you will be saved. For with the heart one believes and is justified, and with the mouth one confesses and is saved. (Rom. 10:9, 10)

- If you have recently taken such an action, <u>please share</u> that with those close to you. Next seek out those you know to be evangelicals (Bible-believing Christians) so they can assist you in getting to know, understand and serve God better.

- Because this plan of salvation <u>excludes good works</u> as a means of being acceptable to God, it is imperative to understand that God does have a plan for ways in which you will serve Him.

> For we are his workmanship, created in Christ Jesus for good works, which God prepared beforehand, that we should walk in them. (Eph 2:10)

May God richly bless you.

APPENDIX
G. ORDER OF END-TIMES EVENT CHART

Rapture   Start of The Tribulation   **Bema Seat Judgment**   **Marriage of the Lamb**
Rescue of Israel   Armies arrayed against Israel destroyed by God   Unholy trinity bound   **Israel converted en masse**   Gathering of the sheep & goats & God's judgment   Tribulation ends   Reconstruction of earth
OT and Tribulation martyred saints resurrected   Millennium begins   **New Jerusalem arrives and hovers over earth**   **Wedding Supper of the Lamb**   **Coronation of Jesus Christ**
Jesus establishes His Temple   **Jesus establishes His world government**   Jesus and saints rule over the Millennium   **1000 years of Christian utopia**   Billions of souls won to Christ
Satan loosed to seduce the unbelievers   Christ destroys rebels/seals Satan's doom
Great White Throne   **New Heaven and New Earth**

BEYOND THE RAPTURE

APPENDIX

H. THEORETICAL GOVERNMENT MODEL

NATIONS JUDGED

One of my challenges to understanding the Millennium has been trying to interpret God's handling of the nations and their rulers at the outset. The nations will be judged at the end of the Tribulation.

In his book, *Things To Come*, Dwight Pentecost gives five arguments against whole nations being admitted to the Millennium. I accept his arguments and will quote but one herein.

"If this judgment is on a national basis whole nations must be permitted to enter the Millennium. Thus, since no nation is made up of all saved people, unsaved would enter the Millennium. Scripture teaches that no unsaved person will enter the Millennium. (cf. John 3:3, Mat. 18:3, and Jer. 31:33–34) …"[1]

In our current world, there are only a handful of countries with kings (or queens) per se. Otherwise, there are presidents, dictators, and *spiritual* potentates leading theocracies (primarily Muslim). There are precious few national leaders who might be Christian and able to enter the Millennium.

Christian mortals entering the Millennium would be *citizens* of particular nations. Such people might very well remain in *their countries* and retain their previous languages and ethnicities. Perhaps this is what is meant by "nations entering the Millennium."

BEYOND THE RAPTURE

RULERS

Another difficulty is discerning how God will integrate the concept of resurrected saints ruling versus mortals ruling. Both concepts are in play.

Furthermore the following scenarios are spoken of:

- The nations will come to Jerusalem to worship Jesus, pay homage and learn of Him.
- These nations will be led by mortal kings who are expected to follow godly principles.

So it is not at all clear how these very differing types of rulership are to be integrated.

When it comes to establishing kings, Jesus could utilize some mixture of resurrected saints and Millennium Christians to rule at the national level. I make this assertion for two reasons. First, certain kings and their nations are shown to be errant during the Millennium. I would not expect this from a resurrected saint who was appointed king. Secondly, in the King James Bible, Christ is said to appoint resurrected saints as kings (cf. Rev. 5:10 NKJ/KJV). Another variation of these ideas is to have mortal kings serve as vassal kings under the authority of Bride Saints serving as kings.

Jesus may appoint promising mortal Christians as kings for certain nations. Each of these kings would then set up his government per Christ's designated paradigm. I am dubious that they would be *kings for life* considering the anticipated long lives of the Millennium.

THEORETICAL GOVERNMENT MODEL

RIGHTEOUSNESS ENFORCED

Having established some of the kingships in the manner described, the Lord Jesus could integrate the righteous Bride Saints as a bulwark against unrighteous acts of Millennium-born kings (or their subjects). So He may require each kingdom to have a Christ-controlled judiciary at significant levels of each kingdom.

> Then I will give you good judges again and wise counselors like you used to have. Then Jerusalem will again be called the Home of Justice and the Faithful City. (Isa. 1:26)

Every king, prime minister, governor, mayor and citizen would be subject to the rulings of this judiciary. In this scenario, the Bride Saints would constitute the majority of the judiciary of every nation. This would provide the righteous (and mandatory) checks and balances needed to keep nations, states and cities on the paths of righteousness.

With such an arrangement, Bride Saints would be *over* governmental agencies at necessary levels. This would be one of the ways that Jesus uses to rule the nations *with a fist of iron*.(cf. Psa. 2:9)

In concert with this would be ecclesiastical structures designed and directed by Jesus. In one way, such a structure might resemble that of the papacy. This hierarchy would probably be manned at the higher levels by Bride Saints. Elders from the churches would fit into this worldwide organization such that Christ is worshipped and served appropriately. This magnificent entity would constitute the most important arm of Jesus' theocracy.

Any such model would exclude Israel, for they will

BEYOND THE RAPTURE

have the governmental structure described in the chapter designated *Israel*. Iraq (ancient Assyria) and Egypt could be directly under Israeli direction or something special as directed by Jesus due to their special dispensation from the Lord. (cf. Isa. 19:23–25)

---

1 Pentecost, 420

APPENDIX

I. COMPENDIUM OF END-TIME VERSES

Many Bible verses which include the phrase "in that day" are commonly interpreted to pertain to the Millennium or the Tribulation. There are also forty-some "in that day" verses which pertain to neither. In certain instances, the phrases "on that day" or "in those days" also pertain (but have not been included).

"IN THAT DAY" VERSES

The following phrases only pertain to the Millennium (or the Tribulation and the Millennium).

NOTE: I have *bolded* certain chapter numbers for ease of reading.

Isaiah 2:1, 17, 20, **4**:1, 2, **10**:20, 27, **11**:10, 11, **12**:1, **19**:16, 18, 19, **25**:9, **26**:1, **27**:2, 13, **28**:5, **29**:18, **30**:23, **32**:5, **33**:6, **52**:6

Jeremiah 30:8–9, **49**:39

Hosea 2:16–18, 21, **3**:5

Joel 3:18,

Amos 9:11–15

Micah 4:1-5, **7**:12

Zephaniah 3:11, 16

Zechariah. **2**:11, **3**:10, **9**:16, **13**:1, **14**:6, 8-9, 16–21

TRIBULATION VERSES

The following "in that day" phrases only pertain to the

BEYOND THE RAPTURE

Tribulation (or the Tribulation and the Millennium):
 Isaiah 2:17, 20, **24**:21, **27**:1, **31**:7,
 Jeremiah 30:8
 Ezekiel 38:18
 Micah 5:9-11,
 Zechariah **9**:16, **12**:3-4, 6, 8-9, 11, **13**:1-2, 4, **14**:4, 13

Another phrase used is "The Day of the Lord"
It is found in:
 Joel 1:15; **2**:1, 11, 31; **3**:14
 Amos 5:18, 20,
 Obadiah 1:15
 Zephaniah 1:7, 14; **2**:2; **14**:1

APPENDIX
J. STUDY OF GOD'S FINAL 3 ERAS

I would hope this book would serve as a primer for those wishing to explore in depth the three eras following The Rapture. Appendices G and I, certain Footnotes and the list of Scriptures utilized should provide assistance in particular and the rest of document in general. Also, utilize the books and internet links in the Bibliography.

The two most helpful books (for me) were Things to Come and The Millennial Kingdom. I also like the website, Truthnet.org (caveat: its wording could use refinement in places). So I encourage those of you so disposed to be good *Bereans* and investigate the Three Eras of God on your own.

ABOVE THE TRIBULATION

The following topics are pertinent to the time between the Rapture and the Millennium:

RAPTURE RESURRECTION

The three resurrections mentioned in the Introduction and Chapter 1 are all part of the First Resurrection. The first one occurs immediately preceding The Rapture.

- Review 1 Cor. 42, 44 & 15:51–53 also 1 The. 4:16-18
- What is the First Resurrection (versus the second)

THE RAPTURE

Please review 1 Cor. 15:52–53 and 1 The. 4:16-17

BEYOND THE RAPTURE

Compare the qualities of the following incidents with the Rapture:
- Jesus' ascension
- Israelites escape thru Red Sea
- Lot's rescue from Sodom and Gomorrah
- Noah and family's escape from the flood
- Elijah's journey to Heaven in a flaming chariot
- Enoch being taken by God.

THE BEMA JUDGMENT

The Judgment Seat of Christ, the Bema, is described in 1 Cor. 3:10-15; 2 Cor. 5:10.

THE WEDDING OF THE LAMB

The Wedding of the Lamb is defined or mentioned in:
- 2Cor, 11:2, Rev. 19:9, Rev.22:17, Mat 25:1, 5. 10

Jesus referred to as the Bridegroom
- John 3:29 and Mark 2:19

Disciples as the friends of the Bridegroom
- Mat. 9:15, Mark 2:19 and Luke 5:34

The Church as the Bride of Christ

NOTE: This topic is similar to The Trinity in that the Church is never specifically mentioned as Christ's Bride.
- The most explicit verse is 2 Cor. 11:2-4. Also see Rom. 7:4 and Eph. 5:22-37

STUDY OF GOD'S FINAL 3 ERAS

RESCUE OF ISRAEL

To understand the why and how of the rescue of Israel, study the following verses:

- Mat. 23:39; Joel 3:9-16, Zec. 13:8-9, Rev. 19:14-31, Rom. 9:27-29, Rom. 11:23-24, Rom. 11:25-27, 30-32

CHRIST'S JUDGMENTS
Review the following:

- Mat. 25:31-46, Rev. 20:10 (Satan & angels), Psalm 7:8, 110:6, Joel 3:12, Isa 66:24, Isa. 2:4, Joel 5:22

RESURRECTIONS

There are two more resurrections to study: The resurrection of OT saints, and the resurrection of Tribulation saints (martyred or otherwise deceased). The martyred saints are mentioned in Rev. 20:4. Bible scholars believe OT saints will be resurrected at the same time.

They deduce this from several passages in the Old Testament: Job 19:25-27; Isaiah 26:19; Daniel 12:1-2. Hosea 13:14 and Ezekiel 37:1-14 describes the regathering of the Nation of Israel using the symbolism of dead corpses coming back to life.

MILLENNIUM

NT BOOK FOCUS

The preponderance of descriptions of the Millennium are found in the OT. That Jesus must repair the Heavens and Earth in preparation is inferred from the devastation wreaked by God during The Tribulation, (cf.. Rev. 6:12–14). There are references to the Millennium sprinkled throughout the NT but the most concentrated text is found in Revelation 20. Recalling other references would be an interesting exercise.

OT BOOK FOCUS

Five OT books provide the greatest focus on the Millennium: Psalms, Isaiah, Jeremiah, Ezekiel and Zechariah.

Jeremiah dedicates three chapters to the Millennium: 30-31, 33.

The following nineteen Psalms are dedicated to the millennial reign of the Lord Jesus and his subjects in the Millennium:

2, 9, 24, 45 – 48, 65 – 68, 72, 96 – 100, 110, 148

Ezekiel provides the timeline for Israel; whereas, Daniel provides the timeline for the Gentiles. Ezekiel describes Israel's future redemption, Christ's temple, and temple worship, activities of the Prince and the River of Life. This begins in Ezekiel 34:11 and continues through the end of the book.

Zechariah describes the Second Advent, aspects of the tribulation and Israel's redemption physically and spiritually. It has been said that Zechariah is the most messianic, apocalyptic and eschatological book in the OT. The chapters addressing these topics are: 1, 2, 8–10, 12–14.

Isaiah gives the most extensive description of the Millennium in large groups of passages. The following

STUDY OF GOD'S FINAL 3 ERAS

chapters pertain to the Millennium in their entirety:

Chapters 4, 11, 12, 35, 52, 54, 55, 60, 61, 62

Now those are the most focused portions of Scriptures, but do recall what I said in the Introduction. All four of the major prophets and nine of the minor prophets address the Millennium. As I said, Jonah, Nahum and Habbakuk are the exceptions.

NEW HEAVENS AND EARTH

Who will be the occupants? Rev. 4:6-10

Why will there be no mortal humans?

Why should the people, flora and fauna and the qualities of the Millennium be included in the eternal state

- See 1 Cor. 15:24-26, 28
- Descriptions: Rev 21:1-7, Isa. 65:17-18, 66:28

Why do scholars believe the New Jerusalem will be integrated onto earth? Start with Rev. 21:3

Examine every place you believe The New Heavens and Earth are described in the Bible.

STUDY APPROACH

You might utilize my topics (chapters and appendices) and accompanying list of Bible verses to frame parts of your study.

You could utilize Appendix I, "Compendium of 'In That Day' Verses" and determine if they are speaking of the Tribulation or Millennium, or simply a shorter-term

BEYOND THE RAPTURE

prophecy.

Also reference the other main Millennium verses and cross reference for other applicable Bible verses.

Review the purposes I list for Millennium (which is far more extensive than anyone I have read). See if you concur. If you disagree, offer Bible proof as to why.

Work to gain an in-depth understanding of what Christ plans to accomplish for and through Israel.

Study about His Prince and see if you concur that it will be David.

See if you can find any other role for David.

Explore temple worship in the Millennium

See what descriptions you can find of Bride Saints' activities as well as Gentile and Israeli mortals in the Millennium.

Study how Christ will deal with rebellion during the Millennium.

There is an excellent set of messages about the Millennium by David Jeremiah. They can be purchased on the internet at www.davidjeremiah.org.

I'm sure you can think of many other ways to investigate the Millennium, but I would challenge you to create a list of purposes and/or desired outcomes (at outset and as you progress).

FINAL THOUGHTS

Do not allow your study to remain purely academic, but allow it to change your perspective and your very life.

APPENDIX
K. MILLENNIUM SONGS

JOY TO THE WORLD

Words by Isaac Watts 1719 (music by G.F. Handel)

Joy to the World , the Lord is come!
Let earth receive her King;
Let every heart prepare Him room,
And Heaven and nature sing,
And Heaven and nature sing,
And Heaven, and Heaven,
and nature sing.
Joy to the World, the Savior reigns!
Let men their songs employ;
While fields and floods, rocks, hills and plains
Repeat the sounding joy,
Repeat the sounding joy,
Repeat, repeat, the sounding joy.
No more let sins and sorrows grow,
Nor thorns infest the ground;
He comes to make His blessings flow
Far as the curse is found,
Far as the curse is found,
Far as, far as, the curse is found.
He rules the world with truth and grace,
And makes the nations prove
The glories of His righteousness,
And wonders of His love,
And wonders of His love,
And wonders, wonders, of His love.

BEYOND THE RAPTURE

ALL HAIL THE POWER OF JESUS' NAME

Text: Edward Perronet; alt. by John Rippon

All hail the power of Jesus' name!
Let angels prostrate fall;
bring forth the royal diadem,
and crown him Lord of all.
Bring forth the royal diadem,
and crown him Lord of all.
Ye chosen seed of Israel's race,
ye ransomed from the fall,
hail him who saves you by his grace,
and crown him Lord of all.
Hail him who saves you by his grace,
and crown him Lord of all.
Sinners, whose love can ne'er forget
the wormwood and the gall,
go spread your trophies at his feet,
and crown him Lord of all.
Go spread your trophies at his feet,
and crown him Lord of all.
Let every kindred, every tribe
on this terrestrial ball,
to him all majesty ascribe,
and crown him Lord of all.
To him all majesty ascribe,
and crown him Lord of all.

APPENDIX

L. THE TRIBULATION: GOD'S PURPOSES, Satan's Plot & Tribulation Events Chart

GOD'S PURPOSES

- Receive The Church unto Himself, reward and marry her
- To judge and punish mankind for their rejection of Christ
- To test the inhabitants of the earth (Rev 3:10)
- To judge and punish mankind for their mistreatment of Christians and Jews
- To bring an end to Satan's rule of earth
- To harvest multitudes of believers even in the face of Satan's heightened persecution
- To populate the Millennium with saved Gentiles & Jews
- To judge yet save the nation of Israel
- To prepare Israel for her Messiah
- To prepare the way for Christ's Millennium

Satan's Plot

- To thwart all God's plans stated above
- To wrest control of earth from God's hands forever
- To establish a brutal world dictatorship
- To trick the world (and especially Israel) into believing that the Antichrist is the promised messiah
- To cause the whole world to worship Satan and his Antichrist
- To destroy Israel and all Jewry from the face of the earth

BEYOND THE RAPTURE

TRIBULATION EVENTS CHART

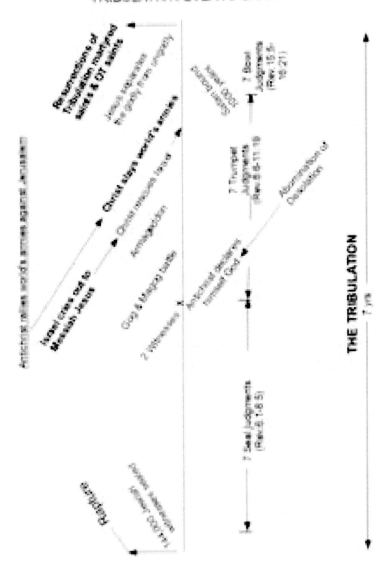

ABOUT THE AUTHOR

Denny Bolen became a follower of Christ in early 1970. He has been married since 1969 and he and his wife, Helen, raised a family of 5 children. They now have 7 grandchildren and 1 great-grandchild. He served as elder for 18 years (in 6-year stints) at Beach Bible Church of Huntington Beach, CA.

He worked with two pastors to lead Evangelism Explosion for several years. He organized a recovery ministry, in which he taught and led various groups (for over 5 years). His professional background was that of a Systems Programmer of large-scale computers and manager in the same arena. He has a Bachelor of Arts from Hastings College, NE. His full name is Earl Dennis Bolen.

He has also published the books, *Recovery Through the Proverbs* and *Christ's Spectacular Millennium*. Incidentally, he also produced a number of technical documents as part of his career in the computing field.

STATEMENT OF FAITH

Denny is an evangelical and concurs with the Evangelical Free Church of America's Statement of Faith (as available on their web site as of January 31, 2012). The web site posting of their statement is available at http://www.efca.org/ about-efca/statement-faith and can be downloaded as a PDF file.

BEYOND THE RAPTURE

ENDNOTES

CAST OF "CHARACTERS"

It is amazing to realize the different people groups that will exist in the Millennium beyond those of different races, nations and languages:

NOTE: Some can qualify for more than one *title,* and some of these designations are mine (simply to help perceptions).

Messianic Bride Saints – Jews who became believers during the Church Age

Millennial Mortals – Mortals who survived the Tribulation or were born during the Millennium

Millennial Saints – Mortals born during the Millennium who accept Christ

Millennial Rebels – Mortals born during the Millennium who reject Christ

Millennial Unregenerate – Mortals who have not yet decided whether or not to follow Christ

New Testament Bride Saints – Believers from the Church Age who are all given the privilege of being the Bride of Christ

New Testament Notables – Spiritually outstanding figures from the Church Age

Old Testament Notables – Spiritually outstanding figures from the Old Testament

OT Prophets – Resurrected, biblically-designated OT prophets

BEYOND THE RAPTURE

Old Testament Saints – True believers from Old Testament times.

Tribulation Survivor Saints – Gentile and Jewish believers who survive the tribulation and enter The Millennium.

Tribulation Martyred Saints – Gentile and Jewish believers who were executed for their faith during the tribulation

Tribulation Jewish Saints – Surviving Jewish believers who were converted en masse by God after Jesus rescued them from certain death (physical and spiritual)

ABBREVIATIONS

AMP – the Amplified Bible

ESV – the English Standard Version

KJV – the King James Version

NES – the New English Standard Bible

NIV – the New International Bible

NKJV – the New King James Version

NLT – the New Living Translation Bible

NT – New Testament

OT – Old Testament

NOTES

Appendix E: The majority of *Ancient Jewish Wedding Practices* is an article written by Burke and Glenna Magee,

ENDNOTES

"Weddings of Ancient Israel. A Picture of the Messiah" (posted on the ReturnToGod.com web site). They have graciously given me a license to reproduce it in this book. I have rearranged parts of it and paraphrased other areas.

Bible Highlights: I have used underlined or bold words in various Scriptures for emphasis.

The New Jerusalem: In Revelation 21:1–8, it appears that God only *fully* reveals the New Jerusalem to earth dwellers after the Great White Throne Judgment (after the Millennium). However most biblical scholars consider that verses 21:9 – 22:7 is a recap of the Millennium and actually the first appearance of the New Jerusalem happens at the beginning of the thousand years.

Statistical Techniques: The technique used to determine the odds of six countries out of 196 countries involved are as follows (cf. Appendix A, Birth Pangs, Israel's Current Dilemma):

Caveat: this is normally expressed with reciprocals (fractional notation) but I am going to forego that to make it easier to comprehend.

- The odds of 1 country out of 196 being named is 1 in 196
- The odds of 2 countries out of 196 being prophesied correctly is 1 in 38,220

    $196*195 = 38,220$

- The odds of 3 countries out of 196 being prophesied correctly is 1 in 7,414,680

    $196*195*194 = 7,414,680$

- The odds of 6 countries out of 196 being prophesied

correctly is 1 in 52.48 trillion

196*195*194*193*192*191 = 5.24789E+13

(Which translated means: 52,478.900.000.000)

The Richter Scale: This earthquake magnitude measurement technique was not introduced until 1931 so I do not know how the earthquakes previous to that time were *put into the mix.*

RECOMMENDED READING

Things to Come, Dwight Pentecost

The Millennial Kingdom, John Walvoord

When a Jew Rules the World, Joel Richardson

GLOSSARY

The abomination of desolation – This event is prophesied to happen at the mid-point in the Tribulation. The anti-Christ will defile the temple by declaring himself to be God. (Mar. 24:15)

The forerunner of this event was when Antiochus IV (Epiphanes), after killing thousands of Jews and committing other terrible atrocities against them, slaughtered a sow on the altar of the temple leading to the Maccabean Revolt (circa 150 BC).

Advent – (from the Latin word *adventus* meaning *coming*) The Second Advent is the anticipated return of Jesus Christ from Heaven. The First Advent was His birth, His ministry, crucifixion, resurrection and ascension.

Agape love – Sacrificial, unconditional love such as God gives (agape is a Greek word).

Amillennialism – The belief that Jesus will not have a one thousand year reign on earth.

Antichrist – the evil individual Satan appoints to dominate the world during the Tribulation. (1 John 2:18)

Baal – A generic reference to one of various gods incorporated into a person's belief system.

Bema seat – A most important event which occurs after the Rapture, when Jesus judges all Church Age Saints for purposes of rewards.

Birth pangs – The analogy Jesus uses to describe the upheavals that occur just before the Tribulation (and to far greater degree during the tribulation) (Mat. 24:8).

Bride of Christ – all believers who trusted in Christ from the time of His resurrection until the Rapture of the church.

Bride Saints – believers who were resurrected or translated in the Rapture and comprise the Bride of Christ.

Catechism – A document providing a summary of the elementary principles of Christianity in question-and-answer form.

End-times – The era just prior to and including The Tribulation and beyond.

European Union – The European Union (EU) is an economic and political union of 27 (currently) independent member states which are located primarily in Europe. The EU traces its origins from the European Coal and Steel Community and the European Economic Community, formed by six countries in 1958. (Wikipedia) web

False Prophet – the third person in Satan's trinity who speaks in a magnanimous manner while promoting the Antichrist (Rev. 16:13).

First Advent – Christ's first appearance: born of Mary, three-year ministry, crucifixion, resurrection and ascension.

Gentiles – All non-Jews

GLOSSARY

Great Tribulation – The second half of the Tribulation, also called "the time of Jacob's trouble," during which God's judgment in wrath is at its peak

Humans – People (mortals) who either enter the Millennium just after the Tribulation or are born during the Millennium

Maranatha – Come, Lord Jesus

Marriage of the Lamb – A mystical eternal union of Jesus and His church at His Second Coming

Marriage Supper of the Lamb – The celebration soon after the *Marriage of the Lamb.*

The Millennium – The glorious 1000-year reign of Jesus Christ following the Tribulation.

Messianic Bride Saints – All Jewish Christians who were raptured or resurrected during the Rapture.

Notable – A person of note (well known for his or her contributions to the causes of God).

Olivet Discourse – This phrase designates Jesus' response to His disciples' question (after He alluded to the destruction of Jerusalem): As he sat on the Mount of Olives, the disciples came to him privately, saying, "Tell us, when will these things be, and what will be the sign of your coming and of the close of the age?": (Mat. 24:3) Because this occurred on the Mount of Olives, it is called *The Olivet Discourse.*

Pandemic – A serious disease which occurs throughout a country, continent or globally.

BEYOND THE RAPTURE

Pax Christus – A term I selected only to make a point (but the actuality of which will be enforced during the Millennium). That is, Jesus will promulgate and enforce peace worldwide.

Pharisees – One of three Jewish religious sects (the other two were the Essenes and Sadducees). The Pharisees were the popular group during Jesus' first advent. They majored on the minors, with the minutia.

Pretribulationalism – Belief that the Rapture occurs prior to the Tribulation.

Premillennialism – Belief that Christ's Second Advent occurs before the Millennium.

Post-resurrection Body – The immortal body given each believer at the Rapture or other resurrection events.

Postmillennialism – The monumentally over-optimistic belief that Christ will not return until the end of a 1000-year golden era on earth wherein, Christianity is predominant worldwide

Posttribulationalism – The belief that the Rapture will not occur until the end of the Tribulation

Progressive Revelation – This is a term which in theological circles refers to the unfolding of God's truths in the Bible (throughout biblical history). In the way I have used the term, I am referring to a phenomenon some theologians have posited. Namely that the entire Bible represents a spiritual courtroom scene, that is, a phenomenon in which God is showing all angelic beings

GLOSSARY

His overall plans and righteousness. *Please reference the Progressive Revelation Appendix B which expounds on this.*

Rapture – That event wherein all NT believers (the living and the dead) are caught up to Heaven with Christ as His Bride (the promised position of all NT saints [cf. 1 Cor.15:51–53, 1 The. 4:14–17]). In some mystical way, the bodies of NT saints who have died are resurrected and integrated with their souls (spirits) which are already with Christ.

Resurrection – Bring back to life after dying.

Replacement Theology – A theoretical position taken by certain Reform Theologians in which they deem the church of Christ as replacing Israel as regards God's promises. More pointedly, they feel God has no further use for Israel or the Jews. Such a position involves abandoning sound hermeneutics in favor of one of anti-Semitism.

Roman Empire – The Roman Empire was the post-Republican period of the ancient Roman civilization, characterized by an autocratic form of government and large territorial holdings in Europe and around the Mediterranean. The term is used to describe the Roman state during and after the time of the first emperor, Augustus. This includes the years from about 44 BC to 1453 AD. (Wikipedia)

Second Advent – The prophesied and anticipated return of Jesus Christ from Heaven followed by the Millennium.

BEYOND THE RAPTURE

Second death – A term meaning sentenced to Hell

Seder – A Jewish ritual feast that marks the beginning of Passover

Sickle – A manual garden implement which usually has a long curved shaft (with one or two handles) and a curved blade almost two foot in length. It is used to mow down grain as well as long grass or weeds.

Survivors – Gentile or Jewish believers who survive the Tribulation.

Synoptic Gospels – Matthew, Mark, and Luke are deemed the Synoptic Gospels because they include many of the same stories, often in the same sequence, and sometimes having the same wording. The word synoptic derives from the Greek *syn*, which means *together*, and *optic* conveying *seen*.

The Tribulation – Two 3 ½ year periods comprising seven years in which God judges the people of earth as described in the book of Revelation. The second half is deemed "The Time of Jacob's Trouble," a time when Israel will suffer greatly.

Tribulation Jewish Saints – Jewish believers who are converted en masse by God after Jesus rescued them from certain death (this is not to say individual Jews will not accept Christ prior to that).

Tribulation Martyred Saints – Gentile or Jewish believers executed for their faith during the Tribulation.

BIBLIOGRAPHY

BOOKS

Alcorn, Randy, *Heaven*, Carol Stream, Illinois, Tyndale House Publishers, Inc, ©2004

MacArthur, John, *MacArthur Bible Commentary*, Nashville Tennessee, Thomas Nelson, Inc, 2005

McClain, Alva J. *The Greatness of the Kingdom*, BMH Books, Winona Lake, Indiana, 2001, bmhbooks.com

Nelson's New Illustrated Bible Commentary

Nashville, Tennessee, Thomas Nelson, Inc,

©1999 (from eBible suite for Palm PDA) 1790 pp

Pentecost, J. Dwight, *Things to Come*, Grand Rapids, MI, Copyright © 1964 by Dwight J. Pentecost, use by permission of Zondervan, 633 pp

Peters, George N. H., *The Theocratic Kingdom*, Grand Rapids, MI; Kregel Publications ©1952, 1972. 3 vols. Used by permission of the publisher. All rights reserved

Pulpit Commentary, The, General Editors: H. D. M. Spence, Joseph S. Exell, publisher: Logos Research Systems, 77 volumes.

Walvoord, John, *The Holy Spirit*. Grand Rapids, MI, Copyright © 1991 by John Walvoord, use by permission of Zondervan

BEYOND THE RAPTURE

Walvoord, John, *The Millennial Kingdom*, Grand Rapids, MI, Copyright © 1959 by John Walvoord, use by permission of Zondervan,

West, Nathaniel, *The Thousand Years in Both Testaments*, .New York: Fleming H. Revell 1880. 493 pp

ARTICLE

Unger, Merrill F. *The Temple Visions of Ezekiel*, Bibliotheca Sacra, 106:48–57, October 1948

BIBLES

The majority of Scripture herein is quoted from the English Standard Bible. I did this due to the overall clarity of this version and Crossway's generous allowance for quotation (without copyright infringement). Any variation from ESV is noted after the quote.

Any underscoring or bolding of Scriptures is done to emphasize the connection to the point being made.

INTERNET

Answers.com, web

Biblegateway.com (source of Scriptures used), web

Bride of Christ, Wikipedia, web

DeYoung, Jimmy, Prophecy Today Weekend,

ProphecyToday.org, web

Haaretz.com (Excerpted from Study: Anti-Semitism in Europe hit new high in 2009, Published 11.04.10, updated

BIBLIOGRAPHY

11.29.11), Tel Aviv University study: By Cnaan Liphshiz, 11/29/11, web

The Hal Lindsey Report, HalLindsey.com, web

Lacunza, Manuel, The Coming of Messiah, Vol. 1, part II, circa 1801 (as transcribed by Jonathan Tillin of birthpangs.org and bannerministries.org.uk) web

Lotz, Anne Graham, Copyright © 2011 Anne Graham Lotz (AnGeL Ministries) Raleigh, North Carolina, USA. Used by permission. All rights reserved,

www.annegrahamlotz.com web

Magee, Burke and Glenna, Weddings of Ancient Israel. A Picture of the Messiah, ReturnToGod.com, by licensed agreement, web

Reuters 28NOV11 web

Scofield, C. I., Wikipedia, web

Truthnet.org, Endtimes, Armageddon and Christ's Return, web

ANCILLARY QUOTE

Elliot, James Personal Journal, 1927 – 1956

BEYOND THE RAPTURE

SCRIPTURE REFERENCES

Introduction

Zec. 12:2a
Mat. 13:43   NLT
Mat. 25:34   NLT
Mat. 27:25
Luke 12:54–56
1 Cor. 2:9b
Rev. 9b–10   NLT
Rev. 20:4–6

Chapter 1 Above the Tribulation

Isa. 14:11
Isa. 14:15–17
Isa 35:5–6
Joel 2:15–16
Joel 2:27
Joel 3:9–16
Zec. 12:10–12a
Zec. 13:1
Zec. 13:8–9
Mat. 25:31–32
Luke 12:48
Luke 14:14   NIV
Acts 2:40–41
Acts 2:47
Rom. 8:23c   NLT
1 Cor. 3:11–15
1 Cor. 6:3
1 Cor. 15:35b–40
1 Cor. 15:42, 44,
1 Cor.15:47, 49, 50b
1 Cor.15:52–53
1 Cor. 15:58
2 Cor. 5:10   AMP
2 Cor. 11:2
Php. 3:20–21   NLT
1 The. 4:16–17
2 The. 1:7-10   NLT
Heb. 6:10–11   NLT
Heb. 8:10   NLT
Rev. 19:6–8
Rev.19:7d–8   NIV
Rev. 19:20
Rev. 20:1–3
Rev. 21:9–11   NIV

Chapter 2 Beginnings

Isa. 25:6   NLT
Dan. 7:14
Dan. 7:22   NLT
Dan. 7:27   NLT
Dan. 10:5–6
Ezk. 36:33c   NLT
Mat. 3:15b–16
Mat. 13:43   NLT
Mat. 25:34   NLT
1 Cor. 2:9b
Gal. 3:6–9   NLT
Eph. 1:9–10
Php. 2:8–11

Heb. 11:10   NLT
Rev. 1:13–16
Rev. 4:2b–8
Rev. 6:12–14
Rev. 11:16-17 NIV
Rev. 14:2–3   NLT
Rev. 19:6–9
Rev. 19:9
Rev. 21:2
Rev. 22:8

Chapter 3 The New Jerusalem

Luke 6:21
Luke 15:10   NLT
John 14:2–3
Heb. 12:22–24b
Heb. 11:13, 15–16
Rev. 21:10b–14 NLT
Rev. 21:11
Rev. 21:15–16
Rev. 21:26–28 NLT

Chapter 4 The Kingdom

1 Kin. 4:24–25 NIV
1 Kin. 4:24–25 NIV
Psa. 47:7–9   NLT
Psa. 96:10–13a
Psa. 96:13c
Isa. 2:2–3
Isa. 4:5–6
Isa. 9:6–7   NIV
Isa. 12:6
Isa. 35:1–2

Isa. 52:1a
Isa. 52:2a
Ezk. 47:1–2
Ezk. 47:6–10a   NLT
Ezk. 47:12b   NLT
Dan. 7:13-14   NIV
Mic. 4:2e   NLT
Zec. 8:2–3   NLT
Zec. 14:16–18
Mat. 7:21a
Rom. 8:19–21 NLT
1The. 2:19   NLT
Rev. 22:1–2

Chapter 5 Bride Saints

Psa. 8:5   NIV
Psa. 65:4   NLT
Psa. 139:14
Isa. 2:3
Zep. 3:17   NLT
Mat. 22:30
John 21:25   NLT
1 Cor. 6:3
1 Cor. 13:13
1 Cor. 15:42–44
Gal. 5:22–23
Eph. 1:18c
Eph. 2:6–7
Php. 3:21   NLT
Heb. 1:14   NLT
Heb. 10:14, 16
1 John. 3:2
Rev. 2:17c

SCRIPTURE REFERENCES

Rev. 19:11–14

Chapter 6 Israel
Isa. 4:2–4, 5-6
Isa. 19:23–25 NLT
Isa. 26:1
Jer. 23:5
Ezk. 36:24–25,:26–27
Ezk. 36:28–30
Ezk. 45:16–17a NLT
Dan. 12:13
Amos 9:15
Hos. 2:14–15a
Hos. 2:15b–16 NLT
Mic. 7:18–20
Zep. 3:9
Zec. 2:11, 12:10
Mat. 8:11 NLT
Heb. 11:13 NIV
Heb. 11:32–33
Heb. 11:37c–38a

Chapter 7 Purposes and Benefits Of The Millennium
Rom. 11:26 NLT
Heb. 4:9–11a

Chapter 8 Worship in the Kingdom
Psa. 145:11–13 NLT
Isa. 2:2b–3
Isa. 11:4
Isa.:11:9

Isa. 35:5-6
Isa. 65:20 NIV
Isa. 66:23–24 NLT
Jer. 31:21
Amos 9:13
Zec. 14:9

Chapter 9 Life in the Kingdom
Gen. 9:2
Psa. 34:7
Psa. 67:1–3a
Psa. 67:5–7
Isa. 2.2
Isa. 2:4c
Isa. 4:5–6
Isa. 9:7
Isa. 11:6–8 NLT
Isa. 14:2c
Isa. 65:18–19
Isa. 66:18c–20
Isa. 23–24 NLT
Hos. 2:18
Mic. 7:11–12 NLT
Zep. 3:9
Zec. 12:10
Zec. 14:16–18 NLT
Luke 15:10
Luke 22:28–30 NLT
Eph. 6:12
Col. 1:16
Rev. 7:9

Rev. 14:20
Chapter 10 Final Events
1 Cor. 15:24–26, 28 NLT
Col. 3:1–4
1 Pet. 4:7–8 NLT
Rev. 20:7–8
Rev. 20:11, 12
Epilogue The New Heavens and Earth
Isa. 65:17-19 NET
1 Cor. 15:24, 28
Rev. 21:4
Rev. 21:10–26
Appendix A Birth Pangs
Mark 13:8 NLT
Appendix B Progressive Revelation
Eph. 1:8b–10
Eph. 3:10 NLT
Rev. 12:10. NLT
Appendix C Mary's Family
Luke 1:30b–32
Luke 1:46b–49 NLT
Appendix D Spiritual Beings
2 Kin. 6:14–17 NLT
Jud. 13:20
Isa. 53:2

Dan. 10:5–6
Mat. 22:30
Luke 9:29 NLT
Luke 16:19–31 NLT
Luke 24:38–43
2 Cor. 5:8 KJV
Col. 2:9 NLT
Appendix E Ancient Jewish Wedding Practices
Mat. 24:36
Luke 22:20
Eph. 1:13–14
Appendix F My Prophesy Testimony
John 3:16
John 10:10b
Luke 21:34–35
Rom. 3:23
Rom. 10:9–10
Rom. 3:23
Rom. 6:23
2 Cor. 13:10
Eph. 2:8–9
Eph. 2:10
1 The. 5:4–6
Appendix H Theoretical Governmental Model
Isa. 1:26

CPSIA information can be obtained
at www.ICGtesting.com
Printed in the USA
LVOW12s1531130717
541250LV00001B/13/P